# Back In Touch
## Wightman Weese

Tyndale House
Publishers, Inc.
Wheaton, Illinois

Scripture quotations are from
the New International Version of the Bible.

First printing, February 1984
Library of Congress Catalog Card Number 83–51072
ISBN 0–8423–0122–4, paper
Copyright © 1984 by Wightman Weese
Printed in the United States of America

*To*

*Phil, Gary, and Isabel, who stood with me in darkest hours.*

*To*

*Jim and Carolyn, who never stopped believing in me.*

*To*

*my wife for life, Priscilla, who never gave up on me,*
*even when I had all but given up on myself.*

# CONTENTS

# PREFACE

When someone is overcome either physically, emotionally, or spiritually, the spark of life and hope sometimes becomes frightfully dim. Perhaps this book will fan that spark into flame in some readers' lives.

It is quite impossible to suffer physically, or emotionally, or spiritually, without one or both of the other areas of our lives becoming involved also. Making a comeback is difficult, because it seems that the weakest part of us, the part suffering the most, has to pull the hardest to get life back on track again.

Spiritual comebacks are often the hardest to make. A Christian may have walked faithfully with the Lord for years, as did David, Jonah, Peter, Aaron, Elijah, and others. Then, one outrageous sin and the saint is in disgrace and defeat.

A so-called "big" sinner, coming out of the world into the church today, often finds himself an instant celebrity. He is sought after to fill pulpits and to give lectures. But a long-time saint who falls into sin and then tries to make a comeback may find doors of ministry closed to him, his talents no longer wanted, and places of service he once filled no longer offered to him.

Perhaps you are one of these unforgiven ones. This book is written for people who want genuine forgiveness, not just sympathy—those who want to make a genuine comeback.

I hope you will not find anything in these pages to make you feel comfortable if you are, in any way, continuing in your disobedience to the Lord. But if you are still in the midst of the struggle, feeling like a failure and feeling defeated, you must be hurting inside. You can come back to God. There is healing.

If I knew you personally, I would want very much to help you. I've known the kind of pain that feels like hot lead being poured into bone marrow. I know that hurting won't stop until you let God help you make a comeback. Cooperate with God or the pain will overtake you again. Right now, if you are depressed about failure, think about the valuable person you are, and how much more useful you will become when you let God help you make your way back to him.

When you have recovered, you will be useful again if you want to be. And you will recognize other hurting people, sometimes intuitively, in ways that you never did before. Other people may view them with unseeing eyes, but you will recognize the kind of pain you used to feel, and you won't condemn them. In the days ahead you may be the person God uses to help them make a comeback too. Then you may even be able to thank God for what you have gone through, and for teaching you lessons you couldn't have learned any other way, for by then you will have been restored. You will be back in touch.

# ONE
# JONAH'S STORY, AND MINE

Jonah must have been ashamed of himself. He had
undergone stress as few humans will ever experience it.
Who can imagine the agony and distress of three days
inside the gullet of a great fish? The pains, the smells, the
continued undulant motion of the sea around him—
stress upon stress. He was so opposed to the mission of
preaching to the Ninevites that it took three days in
the jaws of death for him to change his mind and agree
to go. Perhaps he was hoping death would relieve
him. When Jonah realized that God was not going to
allow him to die, that he would have to stay there
until he agreed to obey, he decided to give up the struggle.

Vanquished, Jonah fulfilled his mission of preaching
to the people of Nineveh, and then he found a nearby
hill from which he could view the coming destruction
of God upon the wicked Ninevites. Evidently he hoped
the people wouldn't repent, then God would destroy
them.

But judgment never came, because God, more loving
than Jonah, was gracious and granted the Ninevites
mercy when they repented.

So angry was Jonah that even a moment of shade

from the hastily grown gourd vine and its just-as-sudden destruction sent him into another fit of rage. God then quieted Jonah's anger with what appears a strange way to end a book, with a dangling, unanswered question. It is the only book of the Bible to end that way, and we may wonder why.

Many of us go through life dodging all the tough questions. Sometimes, like Jonah, we have to suffer before we learn what God is trying to tell us. God isn't restricted to shipwrecks, storms at sea, or deep-sea rides in a fish's belly. He can just as easily use personal failure, a broken relationship, financial reverses, or the loss of a job to speak to us.

In our frustration and anger, we might want to shout back at God as Jonah did, forgetting that even in God's chastening he is more merciful than we. God doesn't always answer all our questions the first time we cry toward heaven or weep our hearts out. But the answers do come, in God's time.

Why did Jonah tell his story? Only Jonah and God knew about the things that happened to Jonah. Yet, Jonah made his story public. We can perhaps understand Jonah's telling about the miraculous rescue from the deep and the three days in the fish. We might understand also the story of his fearless preaching in Nineveh and the tremendous, overwhelming response. That would have made headlines the world over. But it is a bit harder to understand the rest of his report. Why did he tell about such embarrassing personal events?

Who would have known that Jonah had disobeyed God, and that his disobedience had jeopardized innocent lives on board the cargo ship? Who would know that he had had to stay in the fish's belly three days because he had been too stubborn to give in? Who else knew of his childish anger because God had been more merciful than he? And who would not have been ashamed to relate his childish tantrum about the dying gourd vine? But Jonah told all of this.

✗ I began to appreciate Jonah's honesty when it came time to write my own story in the pages of this book. I struggled for months to complete it, wanting to make certain that adequate healing had taken place within me before I sat down to write.

Among the details I had to sift through in my mind were decisions about what should be told and what should be kept secret. I wondered about friends who would read the accounts with an eye for brutal accuracy and the risk involved in turning more people against me who would rather not have known this much about my failures.

Why should I tell so much about myself and all my failures for the whole world to read? There is a point in confessionals at which we all want to say, "Enough!" Too many prayer groups, church testimony meetings, books, and tracts are given over to telling everything that can be known about past sins and failures. Confession in itself, unless it does more than that, has very little value.

If Jonah was anything like me, a real struggle must have taken place between God and him about his decision to "go public." What did it take for Jonah to push through to the end and hand over his story for others to read?

Why would God want Jonah's story written? Ask the thousands, the millions, who have been enlightened by the truths that pour from the pages of his story book.

How many persons through the years have discovered God's mercy and grace offered to people who repent because Jonah obeyed God and preached, and then wrote about it—failures and all! From Jonah we learn that God deals even with disobedient servants and brings them to finish their appointed tasks. From the pages of Jonah we learn that God hates sin. His way of solving the problem of sin is not to help people run away from it or to destroy those who sin, but to help individuals face it, confess it, turn from it and warn others to turn from it. God, who is merciful even when his hand is heavy upon us, will not let us run from him forever.

I hope the readers of these pages will see the theme of forgiveness and grace running through them. More than anything else we need a clearer understanding of God's grace. The Scriptures teach that God is gracious, that he keeps on forgiving and restoring, long after we have given up.

During the days when I was so discouraged, there were times when I thought I would have lost my mind had I not known a sense of God's forgiveness and restoration to usefulness. I would have seen no point in going on. I've learned that God can restore fallen people.

Recently a friend reminded me that failure is an event, not a person. Like Jonah we shrink from telling others of our sins and rebellions against God. And such candor would be foolish if there were no such thing as grace. But for us who dare a comeback, no part of grace is more precious than God's forgiveness, which helps us to forgive ourselves and provides the basis for others to forgive us, if they choose to do so. Most of all, the fact that we are forgiven, restored, and once again useful people in God's sight is the greatest gift of all.

I can't say how it will happen for others. I only know that I needed to rediscover the God who rejoices over sins forgiven; I needed to rediscover the Father who celebrates the return of the prodigal son. I pray that someday all the sons and daughters of God may enter into the joy I felt when he put his arms around me and said, "Welcome home, son. I'm glad you have come back."

# The Lost Axe Head
## (2 Kings 6)

In Second Kings we can almost see Elisha's friend, a student in the school of the prophets, leaving campus with the rest of the work expedition and walking off toward the forest to cut timber for the new building that Elisha and the students were planning to erect.

That school of the prophets must have been something like a modern-day Bible college. A group of young saints would gather around a prophet of God for discipleship training and study of the Scriptures. During those dark days, when the kings of Israel and Judah were turning away from God, the young men of the school of the prophets seemed the only spiritual hope for the future of God's people.

One of the students, using a borrowed axe, was chopping down a tree when suddenly the axe head came off and landed in the nearby river.

That student, probably embarrassed, returned to Elisha and admitted that he had lost the head from the borrowed axe. Elisha asked him to point out the spot where the axe head had fallen. Then, cutting a stick and tossing it into the stream where the piece of iron had sunk, Elisha made the axe head float to the surface. He told the young man to get it, implying that the student was to fix the axe and get back to work.

When I first read that story, I felt pity for the young man who had lost the axe head and with it his usefulness. But after I thought a little longer about what had happened, I felt less sorry for him, because I remembered something about axes from years past.

As a young boy, I was responsible for bringing in the coal and kindling wood for the two stoves that heated our old house in South Carolina. The kindling wood was usually chopped from a pine stump, preferably from a tree cut in winter when all the sap was concentrated in the roots. The hard, resinous wood was ideal for lighting coal fires.

The pine stumps were tough and hard to chop. From those old stumps I learned about axes and axe heads. Before an axe head is anywhere near loose enough to fall off, a certain vibration can be felt every time the axe bites into the wood. It was possible to keep chopping, even after the telltale vibrations, but I knew that if the heavy blade were to slip off the handle, it would endanger the life of whoever was in range. I knew I must stop the first time I felt the head loosen and pound another wedge of wood or metal into the end of the handle to tighten the head.

I think it is possible that Elisha's young servant knew the axe head was loose and just failed to do anything about it. The fact that it was a borrowed tool may also have accounted for his being so careless.

For whatever reason, the servant's usefulness was gone with the lost blade. Perhaps he stood there, thinking about the telltale vibrations he had ignored. What an embarrassment!

Elisha told the young prophet, "Take it up to yourself." God worked a miracle to make the young man useful again. It was important to know where the tool had fallen, to know how he had lost his usefulness. It was important for the young man to get it back and start to work again.

I think I can see that young prophet at work again, cutting down the tree he had started to fell. Is he praying as he works, thanking God for a good sharp axe? Does he remember that the axe is borrowed and that it took a miracle to get it back? That tool is especially precious to him now, because for a while he thought it was gone forever—a total loss. He's thanking God for the miracle that brought it back.

I can imagine that every now and then he pauses to see if the wedge in the head of the axe is tight enough so he won't lose it again. He's much more sensitive now to the vibrations he overlooked before. I can imagine he stops occasionally to warn his friends working alongside him to be careful.

He still looks a little embarrassed and seems to be working a bit faster than the rest, as if trying to make up for the time he lost. Perhaps he will always be a little ashamed of what happened to him, but he seems so happy to be back on the job again that getting the job done is more important than the memory scars that he will probably always bear.

# TWO
# **STUMBLING**

My family and I were in and out of church until my senior year of high school, at which time I received Christ into my life during an evangelistic crusade. The next years were a constant struggle with feelings of guilt for past sins and inability to do very much about such habits as a bad temper, smoking, profanity, to name just a few. Poorly instructed, not fully understanding what the Christian life was all about, I was making no apparent spiritual progress.

During two years in the Army, away from my church and family, my early childhood values dissipated in the coarseness of military life. It was at Columbia Bible College several years later that I first understood what Christ's life in me was supposed to do for me. My father suggested I go there, and somehow I too felt it was God's direction for me. I struggled with school rules, trying still to break out of old habits, questioning during these struggles if I had made the right choice after all. God's plan for me became clearer when he led me to the girl God had chosen for me. Priscilla's sweet, strong spirit, her love for God, and her desire to serve him made me want very much to be a part of her life, to learn to love God as she did.

We were married before my junior year at college, and shortly after graduation, we left for Africa to work in missionary medical and education ministries. Our third child was born a few months after our fifth anniversary, just six months after we arrived in Africa. After two overseas terms we returned to America so I could enroll in studies for a master's degree in preparation for a third term overseas. As it turned out, we never got back to Africa.

The exhausting struggle to complete thirty graduate credits in journalism in two semesters made a different person out of me. Something happened that year that changed my whole attitude on life.

One day on campus, playing my usual role of missionary-clergyman, I jokingly criticized a student for using some bad language while talking on the phone to me. As a result, the girl was too embarrassed to come to the same class with me the next day. Then I remembered, as I was apologizing to her, that I had used the same words in the privacy of my garage several days earlier when my car wouldn't start. I realized what a phony person I was becoming, trying to project the image of righteousness to this girl while being another person alone in my garage. A wave of remorse swept over me. I was trying to introduce this girl to the Lord, but I had showed nothing of Christ to her. All she saw was harsh judgment that I wasn't applying even to myself.

I hated myself and the hypocrisy I had shown, the kind of artificial spirituality that was becoming a way of life for me. That glimpse of myself made me sick. Not only was such playacting not effective in presenting Christ, it was making a dishonest person out of me.

I think now that being so physically tired and emotionally drained from the heavy study schedule caused the incident to depress me more than it otherwise would have. For whatever reason, I've been grateful to the Lord

for allowing that experience to weigh so heavily on
me. It was the jolt I needed to start doing something
about my life. I began to pray for God to make me
genuine, inside and out.

I wasn't really prepared for all the changes that came
when I prayed that prayer. I wasn't happy with the
things I began to learn about myself. If the Lord could
make me what he and I wanted me to be, I realized I
could quit pretending to others and also quit deceiving
myself about what I really was like.

It was a liberating experience. In those last few months
in graduate school I made my first genuine attempts
to be the same person inside that I was seen to be outside.
It became easier to own up to failures, easier to pray
for grace to change, easier to forgive and accept the
failures of others. Becoming transparent also humanized
my testimony. Before, I had told people about the
Lord. Now I could tell them about a relationship with him
that I was actually experiencing. I began to see results
that I had only dreamed about before. People seemed to
have a different and more meaningful respect for me
when I owned up to my humanness. Honest about my
spiritual ups and downs, I was no longer a threat to
other people, so they felt safe with me and trusted me
with their inner thoughts and struggles. It was a strange
but exciting new experience in usefulness.

For the next three years, as a teacher at a Christian
college, I became involved in a fruitful counseling ministry
with students. Because of what the Lord had done in
my life, the students began to open up their lives to me.
It was an extremely gratifying experience, but I soon
began to wonder if I was feeling gratified because of the
useful ministry or because of the thrill that came to
me from feeling needed. In other words, was I ministering
from a life of wholeness or was I ministering to meet
some need of my own, a desire to be needed? There is

no feeling to compare with the sense of being used of God. It will cause a person to work for a pittance and undergo personal hardships of all kinds. It can even blind some people to the dangers of such a vulnerable position.

One of my Bible teachers, Dr. Frank Sells, used to warn his students to be especially wary of Satan's attacks, noting that when God gave him some special victory or taught him some special lesson, he should be prepared for a specific attack of Satan, challenging him in the very area where he thought he had won his biggest victory.

It wasn't the first time I had questioned my motivation for working with the students and the good feelings I got from it. One of the college psychology professors had dropped by my office to commend me for spending time talking with some of the troubled students. I suppose he thought I was, in some way, lightening his heavy counseling load. At the time, the college didn't have a campus chaplain, so a number of the professors found themselves involved with students who were looking for help.

I told him how much I enjoyed such a ministry with students and then sought his opinion: "Am I in it for what I'm getting or for what I'm giving?"

He tried to reassure me. "Do you think God would have you spend so much time with these kids if you didn't enjoy it? Do you think you could help them if you didn't like them and didn't enjoy what you're doing?"

I left it at that, but he really hadn't answered my question. I wanted him to tell me whether or not my desire to extend myself to students was a symptom of some basic need that I felt wasn't being met in any other way, perhaps by my parents as I was growing up, or by my wife and family, or by others.

The purist in me argued that I must be properly motivated or nothing I did was really worthwhile. The other part of me, the pragmatist, answered, "What difference does it make if some of your motives can't be fully analyzed? What you are doing is working. You are getting results. Students are responding positively and their lives are changing for the good. And they are praising the Lord for the changes. Why worry as long as what you are doing is working?"

I couldn't understand why certain students were drawn to me and I to them. Many of their problems defied analysis. Most were from good homes and had loving parents. Yet many of them acted as if somewhere along the way they had been emotionally traumatized. I'm sure that some of my concern for them was God's love working itself out through me, because I don't know how I could have loved some of them otherwise. They were irritable, obstinate, sometimes even rude. But that was, I realized, only symptomatic of their problems. The Lord gave me a special love for them, which was just the kind of encouragement that many of them needed to see themselves as being of value. As a result, they understood God's love a little better and began to accept themselves and the changes that the Lord was working in them.

But the time came when most of these students whom I had come to care for and love so dearly began to grow strong again. Many were a little embarrassed that they had needed me and the emotional and spiritual crutch that my concern for them had provided during the times they were struggling through their hurts. I had to be careful to keep their secrets. Some of them must have feared that I might fail them by telling about some of the dark places of their lives that they, in their moments of weakness, had exposed to me.

When the time came for them to go their way, I always felt a sense of loss, much like a parent whose children leave the nest. I had become overly subjective in my love for them, and when it was time to become objective again, it always hurt me a little. I somehow felt like a castoff, not being needed by them anymore. Perhaps that feeling was a danger signal I should have been heeding, a signal like the vibrations coming through the axe handle.

As time went on, I became a little better able to manage the situation in which such friendships with the students were formed. The counseling sessions were time-consuming, but I felt them a necessary part of doing a good job as a professor on a Christian college campus.

Yet, during those busy days, some unhealthy signs began to surface in my family life. It was becoming difficult for my wife and children to understand the long hours I spent away from home, or the frequent trips back to campus to spend time with a student who was in trouble. I thought I was making a special effort to spend time with my wife and children, but there just didn't seem to be enough of my time to go around.

During those frustrating days an offer came that I hoped would solve some of our family problems. I gave up teaching for a position in publishing, a position which seemed at the time to offer a more profitable future.

I was almost glad to leave campus, eager to be free from the frustration of mixed emotions and motivations.

But the change in scenery didn't eliminate the problem. The same interest in people was still there. I didn't lose my sensitivity to those in emotional or spiritual distress, even when they sometimes tried to mask it. "How did you know?" many people asked me when I would confront them about something I sensed was going wrong in their lives. For a long time I really didn't understand why I was sensitive to people who were hurting inside, or why I seemed to detect signs often before the person himself was willing to admit it. When I would probe a bit, I discovered that these insights were nearly always correct. Believing it was the Holy Spirit developing these insights within me, I began to rely on them.

Later, when questions about my motivation arose, I realized that part of the reason for this sensitivity to people who felt unloved or depressed or those who were searching for meaning, was that I too was feeling unloved, depressed, and was sometimes having difficulty finding meaning in life.

As a child I used to open the front of our old upright piano and loudly sing a certain note. Then I would be silent and listen to the piano strings as they picked up the harmonics set up by my shout. The note would resonate for a few seconds on the piano strings, the same pitch that I had sounded with my voice. In somewhat the same way, I was seeing some of my own pain in the faces of those I encountered. Their needs and emptiness were striking resonant notes in my own life. The tenderness I was feeling for them was the tenderness I subconsciously sought for myself. I was finding it in the people to whom I was giving it, and it was this response that got me into trouble.

During the next two years, three of my friends came to the brink of divorce. In each case, I allowed myself to be drawn into their concerns. Each of these friends, dependent upon me for a time, also walked away, keeping their marriages intact. For a time they seemed to need my encouragement and help, but when they got better they didn't need me anymore. Each marriage that was straightened out became a sort of spiritual victory for me. Yet each time I felt abandoned when I was no longer needed.

The nagging questions returned: "Why are you getting involved again? Why you, and not someone with the proper credentials? You're not a psychologist or a trained counselor. What signals are you sending out that make them think you are someone they can approach? You just have to be needed, don't you?" The purist and the pragmatist within argued over and over again.

What was this strange, inexplicable sensitivity to depressed, demoralized, and spiritually exhausted people? I began to spend more and more time meeting people, to the point where I had to start asking them to come to my home, or I would go to theirs, because seeing these couples was absorbing too much of my work time. I had no hobbies—golf, tennis, or social clubs—nothing beyond church activities. The rest of my time was spent with my family and these friends. One week I spent more than twenty hours with one young couple, trying to help them, encouraging them to seek professional help for a problem that was beyond me.

These meetings with people were all taking time away from my family, who were coming to accept my counseling as a way of life. Sometimes I wondered if my wife and family were really getting a fair share of my time, but then the good feelings and sense of service and usefulness that I was getting from others dimmed my sensibilities in that direction.

Later, since I wasn't always available to them, my family lost some of their enthusiasm for what I was doing. Yet, since I wasn't initiating any of these outside contacts, I felt justified in keeping my door open. "I'm no psychologist," I told my family. "Do you think I have a shingle hanging over my door?"

These friends knew I was an ordained minister, and it was probably because I wasn't a psychologist that they came, knowing I was no threat to them, their church relationships, or their jobs. Since they came to see me as friends, their other friends didn't have to know why they were coming.

Self-pity became a terribly destructive attitude for me at this point in my life. Because others were so grateful toward me, and my family at home seemed not to understand, I began to believe the lie that I wasn't really loved and respected at home as much as I was by others outside the home.

Then it happened. One of the people who appeared on the scene, needing help and spiritual counsel and finding it, didn't walk away. She asked to stay. If she had misunderstood my concern, others who knew us both also misunderstood what our relationship was. I did love her, but it was as a child of God and as a sister in the Lord. Yet, almost unconsciously, I was wanting it to become more than that, to the point where she became emotionally confused. How quickly my good intentions dissipated. And I too allowed my emotions to go to shreds.

Rather than helping her, I ended up hurting her and the thought of that was too much to bear. The knowledge that I had come to love someone beyond what was legitimate in God's sight filled me with a sense of guilt as profound as if the most personal intimacy had taken place. Because I handled the situation so poorly, my usefulness ended as surely as the axe head had disappeared from the handle that Elisha's friend held useless in his hand.

Once there had been a time when my greatest goal was to acquire enough money and creature comforts to take care of myself, my family, and all my friends for life. Later, after I became a Christian, I wanted to be the most successful missionary or pastor that I could possibly be, someone who would make a great name for himself in the ministry. But at last the time came when to me the greatest good, the only thing I felt worthy of any effort, was to be a useful tool in God's hand to help others. Now that too seemed to be gone, forever.

Why hadn't this last encounter turned out as well as all the others? How could anything that started with such good intentions turn out to be so bad and painful? What

had I done wrong that now left me so embarrassed
and with such feelings of uselessness? I had to have
answers, or I couldn't go on.

Loving others certainly isn't wrong. Love is one of the
primary marks of a Christian. The Bible is filled with
commands to love. Holiness of life is the other command
believers are given. How had I managed to allow my
love for another to draw me into a situation that gave
others the impression that I had compromised myself.
Loving people in the right way is a spiritual work. Loving
them the wrong way would have to be called the work
of the flesh that Paul wrote about: "So I say, live by the
Spirit, and you will not gratify the desires of the sinful
nature" (Gal. 5:16).

I know that I could never attempt to minister to anyone,
trusting in my own abilities, or in my past record of
"success," or in anything that would hinder the Spirit's
work through me. The fact that God had used me
in some situations as an effective tool didn't mean that I
could plunge undirected into other situations and
expect the same success.

When the young worker turned to Elijah for help, he
cried out, "It was borrowed." Of course it was borrowed!
All of our real effectiveness is borrowed. We possess
nothing that God can use that is not given to us by the
Holy Spirit. Our lives are little more than axe handles,
totally useless apart from the sharp cutting axe head
that the Holy Spirit is within us. But through carelessness
comes neglect, and then our usefulness is gone.

Paul wrote, "But we have this treasure in jars of clay to
show that the all-surpassing power is from God and
not from us" (2 Cor. 4:7). Of course, we must cooperate
with God as he works in us to minister the gospel to
others. But he does the effective work as long as we don't
get in the way and try to take the credit, or try to serve
ourselves along with trying to serve others. My problem,

I realized, was that I was unconsciously using the ministry God gave me to meet my own selfish needs, and it didn't work.

Is such sensitivity all bad? Aren't some of our troubles to prepare us to minister to others? Paul said that the comfort God had given him was to make him effective in the lives of others who suffered as he had suffered. "God . . . comforts us in all our troubles so that we can comfort those in any trouble with the same comfort we ourselves have received from God" (2 Cor. 1:4).

I had to discover the hard truth that such empathy must not rise from self-pity. A person who has grown "weary in doing good," as Paul cautioned believers not to do, and begins to feel sorry for himself, can't be much help to anyone else. As long as I was loving unselfishly, the Lord was using me; the moment I became concerned about my needs, I failed.

I should have chosen to commit that unfulfilled desire to be loved by others to the Lord and allowed him to comfort me in his own way. I could have ministered that kind of comfort to others. Instead, I accepted comfort from the wrong source. I was, in effect, saying that God's comfort to me was no longer good enough.

The worst damage being done was perhaps the hurt I was bringing to my wife. She had genuinely loved me all along, but some deep personality scars inside me, yet undealt with, were making me feel unloved. In such a low spiritual and emotional condition, there probably wouldn't have been enough people in the world to make me feel loved. No wonder I was failing!

# THREE
## THE ATTRACTION

As soon as I saw her in the crowded room I knew
something was wrong. Her usually neat clothes were
disheveled as were her hair and makeup. Usually
such poor grooming reflects that something is wrong
internally, so I immediately began to pray. Later I heard
that there was trouble in her home.

When we happened to meet again at a business
meeting, she told me what was wrong. I told her that I
had been praying, and she asked if I knew that her
husband was divorcing her. She'd had an affair, her
husband had discovered it, and there had been a terrible
scene.

The shame of having been found out was the most
damaging consequence as far as her future was concerned.
That she had to struggle with the fears of a mental and
emotional collapse was the immediate concern. When a
person allows something so inordinate to happen to
himself or herself, the loss of self-assurance is staggering.
"How in the world could I have been so stupid as to
allow this to happen to me? I simply can't believe I've
done it: I must be losing my mind," she said, over
and over.

The fear of losing her husband and family, not to mention her relationship with her father, a well-known man in Christian circles, was also tearing her apart.

But the biggest grief for her seemed to be the feeling of death hanging about her. The man with whom she'd had the affair, who was to her a dear, tender, caring person, was gone, as if he had really died. Knowing she would never see him again was a pain worse than death. It would almost be easier to see his casket being lowered into the ground. At least a real death of the man she loved might be handled more easily.

However he was not dead, but alive, out there somewhere, probably in as much pain as she was. She would always remember his eyes, his smile, the tenderness of his touch.

She mourned a death, just as real as the kind drenched in sympathy cards and flowers. But it was much worse because there were neither flowers nor sympathizing friends. She was denied even a proper mourning of her loss, the death of a relationship.

No one dared show any sorrow for her, because it was a relationship that never should have been. People might think that offering her sympathy was the same as condoning her sin.

For his love she had been willing to sacrifice everything. And now, having lost that love, she felt she was losing everything else as well—everyone and everything that could help to fill the void. She had no business, no right, to fall in love with a man who was not hers to have. Even her friends found it hard to offer her comfort, no matter how much she was grieving.

Words are inadequate to describe the life that has lost its object of love. The soul seems to develop a huge cavity. Everything within the chest walls seems suddenly gone. The sufferer sees a face in the mirror but can't seem to recognize it. So dependent for his or her own

identity on the departed one, the sufferer sometimes
becomes a stranger to himself. Part of the loss is the
accompanying feeling that hope has died also. The
unholy love was blasphemy enough. Such a person would
feel a deep reluctance to call on God for comfort from
the pain caused by giving up a sinful love, since the
relationship should never have existed in the first place.

And somewhere out there he was probably feeling
the same way. I knew who he was, but didn't know him
as well as I knew her. But when I happened to see
him a few weeks later, even from a distance I could read
the pain on his face.

Rarely had I seen a more disintegrated life than I saw
in this woman. She was already seeing two counselors, a
psychologist, and a pastor. I recommended yet another.
But no counselor can do what God alone can do.
Doctors and psychologists cannot really enable a person
who is pulverized by feelings of guilt to stop feeling
guilty, as one of her counselors was trying to tell her to
do. She felt guilty because she *was* guilty.

David once prayed, in words only those who have
been reduced to that kind of remorse can fully appreciate:

*O Lord, do not rebuke me in your anger or discipline me
in your wrath. For your arrows have pierced me, and
your hand has come down upon me. Because of your
wrath there is no health in my body; my bones have
no soundness because of sin. My guilt has overwhelmed
me like a burden too heavy for me* (Psalm 38:1-4).

Doctors can give sleeping pills and medication for
nausea. Counselors can try to keep people from committing
suicide or from thinking they are losing their minds, but
only God can remove guilt.

This woman needed to understand God's forgiveness
and that no sin was so great that it couldn't be forgiven.

"God doesn't hear my prayers any more," she said. The words frightened me. I had heard them only once before, from a retired missionary lady who had been a great influence on my life when I was growing up. Old and senile, living in a nursing home, she had become mentally confused and thought God had abandoned her. "I can't get through to God. He's deserted me," she sobbed.

But I had seen too much of her faith and trust in action when I was growing up. The only thing that had changed for her was her physical condition. God was as close to her as he had always been. Later, when doctors changed her medication, her mind cleared up and her joy in the Lord returned. But her remarks that day taught me an important lesson. When, for whatever reason, a person loses the sense of God's presence, I believe that person's anguish is just as great as if the Lord had in fact abandoned him or her.

The woman I was trying to minister to was, as far as she was concerned, forsaken by God, alienated from her family and husband, and disgraced in the eyes of her friends.

How was she, and the hundreds of men and women like her, going to recover? Where were her friends, those courageous enough to counsel her when the problem began? Had Satan trapped her so suddenly that she had no chance whatever?

What were the danger signs that her husband should have seen to point out how vulnerable she was to such an attack of Satan? The man involved was a well-known Christian in the community, someone who should have been helping her instead of hurting her. Being a leader was no guarantee that his associations with her would be without consequences if their relationship got out of bounds, as it eventually did.

Confronting sin is an unpleasant job. The Corinthian

church found it difficult. The story of the man and his stepmother shows that. When we read the brief reference to that episode in 1 Corinthians 5, we usually think of it as a sordid, physical thing which it obviously came to be. But it is hard to believe that it was only a physical relationship. Something strong was at work to bring two people into such a relationship that made them willing to stand against the whole Body of believers in Corinth. Their insistence as to the rightness of their relationship evidently caught the weak church so off guard that no one challenged them.

Could this couple have been reasoning that something which brought them such delight could not come from anyone but God? Others have used that excuse. Paul had preached "love one another" to them until they were glad to hear someone even peripherally agreeing with them about their feelings.

Corinth, the city of erotic love, probably had its influence on both of them. We know nothing of the age of these two, or how it could be that a man would become involved with his father's wife. Because the affair was so well known, Paul felt no need to explain the details. The facts were clear enough to the people to whom he was writing the letter.

From the context it appears to have been more than just a one-time affair. It was an ongoing relationship, well known to the community, one which the couple evidently planned to continue.

All kinds of reasons could have been given for continuing the relationship. They may have been using some excuses frequently reiterated in our day.

"Neither of us was happy where we were." When someone is missing intimate love in his life, it is easy to start thinking irrationally, and to say, "I must be loved and cared for by someone, no matter what it costs me."

"We never intended to start caring so much for each

other," others say. Very few such people do. The fact
that they were careless about the circumstances in which
the sharing began seems irrelevant at the moment.
Some people at such a time want to hold God responsible
for "allowing them to fall in love." If a relationship with
someone is not legitimate, obviously God didn't intend for
the relationship to start. But people who fall in love
often want to blame God for the fact that they were in
the wrong place at the wrong time.

Paul's letter to the Corinthians gave no detail of why
this affair began, and his letter gives us little about
why the church had allowed it to continue unchallenged.

Paul said that the couple, especially the man, was
wrong. Because of the cultural situation, it appears that
the man was considered more responsible for what
had happened.

Paul didn't blame the church for the fact that the
relationship occurred, but he clearly blamed them for
allowing it to go on. They were conceited, puffed up with
pride, not because of the sin, but in spite of the sin,
Paul told them. The Corinthians were glorying in their
gifts, oblivious to the cancer of sin in their midst. It
was their indifference that Paul was addressing, their
chasing after the gifts of the Spirit instead of the fruit of
the Spirit, seeking for what the Spirit could do among
them and not what he wanted to do in them.

The man and his stepmother should have known the
relationship was doomed from the start because it
had no foundation on which to build. They both knew it.
All their friends probably knew it, though they said
nothing. In a way, it was probably a relief when Paul's
letter arrived even though the public reading must have
been a terrible experience for all of them.

The church leaders calling the man to the side after the
meeting, the hurt and angry look on his face would
probably have been enough to punish the woman involved,

even though Paul's letter said nothing specifically to
her. It might have been considered punishment enough
for her to know that her lover was receiving public
rebuke.

The story of the Corinthian man and woman tells the
story of hundreds each year who fall into the same
deceptive trap. It is a story as old as the Church.

Christians are genuinely concerned when such scandal
hits the Church, but unfortunately congregations today
seem almost as inept as the Corinthian church to deal with
errant brothers and sisters, not only in confronting them
but in restoring them when they repent and try to return
to the fellowship.

Paul described how much easier they found it to allow
themselves to go to unbelievers for judgment rather
than to allow the church leaders to judge between them.
It seems they didn't like to call each other "sinner."
Such a distorted view of love may have been the reason
Paul gave such a full treatment of genuine love in
chapter 13 of his first letter to them.

Perhaps they thought Christian love meant "be nice,
be sweet, don't tell anybody he is wrong." But one of the
most loving things any of them in the Corinthian church
could have done would have been to go to the man
or woman and say, "What you are doing is wrong. Please
don't continue it. I don't want God to have to punish
you. Confess it and God will forgive you, and we'll forgive
you too."

The problem facing the Corinthian church has not gone
away. Like them, we often fear to confront other
members of the Body about what is wrong, because we
don't want to offend. Perhaps it is because we don't
know what to do to make things right again once a person
has confessed the sin and repented. Could it be that
we don't judge one another and call sin by its right name
because we wouldn't know how to forgive and restore

the person once we have dealt with his sin, once the person has confessed it and forsaken it?

It is hard to say how much time elapsed between the writing of First Corinthians, in which Paul told them to deal with the errant ones, and the second letter. Perhaps it was as much as a year.

From 2 Corinthians 2:5-11, we gather that someone was aware of what was happening to the man and had kept Paul informed. Paul's letter told the Corinthian church what they needed to do. They were to forgive the man and they needed to comfort him to see that he grieved no more than was necessary.

When my wife was a child, an argument broke out between her and her younger sister. Tired of hearing them argue, their father shouted, "Hey, you two! Bury the hatchet!"

"OK," her sister said, and then whispered, "But I'm gonna leave the handle sticking out."

How much does genuine forgiveness include? To a known bank embezzler, does it mean giving him another chance at the money till? To what degree does a sin brought to light indicate a basic incorrigible character flaw which should not be trusted again in the same place of responsibility?

It is easy for us to ask tough questions about sin, forgiveness, and restoration. It is another thing to see genuine restoration put into effect.

A friend of mine, who as a young man had quite an exciting ministry to the young people in his congregation, was introduced to one of the girls in the church. She had become engaged to someone her parents considered beneath her socially, so the parents set about trying to break up their romance. The parents finally succeeded, and then quickly started pushing the girl toward the part-time youth director.

She was cute, a Christian, and her parents were very

nice, so the youth director took an interest in her. Soon they were married, but in a short time she became unhappy. She said she was still in love with the fellow her parents disliked. Soon she set out to destroy her marriage and eventually her health. She had a medical problem that required her to take daily medication, but she started skipping it on purpose. She started overeating and was soon about forty pounds overweight. Threats of suicide followed. A child was born, but then a few months later that youth leader and his wife were separated and later divorced.

Of course, the youth director's ministry in that part of the country was ended. Except for some behind-the-scenes activity, he had little ministry at all. Several years later he remarried, and I hope by now he has found genuine recovery and restoration. But I believed then, and still do, that the forgiveness others show him will be as important to his recovery as his own efforts. Paul said, "Ye ought to forgive . . . him." The youth director is back in church now, but not quite all the way back. Even though he is the "innocent party" in his original marriage failure, if there is such a thing as an innocent party, he is still not ministering publicly anymore.

Another friend of mine, who was caught in an indiscreet situation with a woman friend, is back in church, but not all the way back. His creative skills once had an impact in a Christian outreach ministry. But I doubt if he will ever again hold such a position in another organization. He is almost forgiven, almost comforted, but not quite restored.

Why comfort and forgive anyone? "So that he will not be overwhelmed by excessive sorrow . . . in order that Satan might not outwit us, for we are not unaware of his schemes" (2 Cor. 5:11).

The real question is, what are Satan's schemes? Is it to keep people in a state of unforgiveness?

We must all answer for ourselves whether or not there
is such a thing as a second-class Christian, one who
has had a chance at respectability, but lost it through
personal sin. If all are sinners, and God can forgive
all of us, yet some of us cannot be forgiven by other
sinners, then something is wrong.

Some of those I know who have faltered and fallen
have struggled with temptations the "first-class Christians"
will perhaps never know. It is hard to expect such
people not to be tempted to bitterness when fellow
believers can't or won't receive them again.

We evangelicals preach many messages aimed at
conviction, but not many on comfort. The people we
would most readily convict are often the ones already so
overwhelmed by a sense of sin and guilt that they
despair of recovery, of anyone's forgiveness.

The Holy Spirit is the Paraclete, the one "called
alongside." His ministry is twofold, to comfort when
comfort is needed and to convict when sin is present. We
also must learn how to do both, to bring comfort as
well as conviction.

Many discouraged, beaten-down people still seem to be
waiting for Paul's second letter to arrive, telling people
how to forgive and comfort overwhelmed people. I try to
tell them that it is coming. Some of them point to me
and say, "Has it come for you?" Perhaps not completely,
I must answer. Some never seem to understand
forgiveness. But we must be patient. It is coming. For
everyone's sake, I hope the letter arrives soon.

# Aaron
## (Exodus 32;
## Leviticus 16)

Outside the tabernacle stood a crowd, waiting to see if a
man could stand in the presence of God and live.
Inside stood a fearful priest, aware of his own sinfulness
and past rebellion. He was Aaron, the High Priest,
God's chosen mediator between himself and his people,
Israel.

It was the solemn Day of Atonement. Jeweled and
heavily embroidered garments of the High Priest were
laid aside on this special occasion. Today he wore only a
simple priest's garments.

The offerings had been carefully selected. With great
attention Aaron had washed himself, slain the bullock
according to the laws, and set aside the sin offering and
the scapegoat which would be released later. Now,
behind the veil, Aaron was bringing coals from the altar,
some of the blood of the offering, incense, and part
of the meal offering to sprinkle before the Mercy Seat of
God.

Did Aaron's hands tremble? Were his thoughts on his
two sons so recently slain by the fire which came from
God? One of these sons, had he lived, would have been
the next High Priest.

One can only imagine Aaron's anguish over the death of Nadab and Abihu. In their zeal to be a part of the priesthood, they had taken careless liberties with the laws of sacrifice and worship. Because of their disobedience, God smote them when they brought their improvised offering to him. By this terrible object lesson the holiness of God was demonstrated for the benefit of all the people.

Love and fear mingled heavily within Aaron's spirit at the thought of standing before such an awesome God. To free Israel from Egyptian bondage God had worked great miracles. Yet, how severely he had punished Israel each time they strayed from him! When Israel obeyed him, he blessed them. When they rebelled against Moses, God punished them with bitter waters one time, with serpents another time.

We can almost hear Aaron's heart pounding as he parted the heavy curtains to enter the Holy of Holies. Would he live to tell of his moments before God?

Meticulously washed and anointed, robed in white linen clothing, sash, and turban, Aaron entered. Those washed hands that carried the censer and vessel of blood were the same hands that several months earlier had crafted the golden calf which the Israelites had foolishly worshiped, an act that caused God's anger to break forth, destroying three thousand people.

For the rest of his life Aaron would have to live with the knowledge that his decision to give in to the pressure of the people to fashion the golden calf had resulted in the deaths of three thousand people.

Aaron would have to answer to his own conscience as to whether or not the people would have debauched themselves had he not given in to their wishes. God had not failed them in any way. Why couldn't Aaron have waited and urged the people to be patient for a little longer?

How much of Aaron's impatient spirit, his unwillingness
to attend to detail as demonstrated by the golden calf
incident, had rubbed off onto his sons so that they also
disobeyed? Again Aaron had no reply. He was silent,
as if afraid even to grieve for his dead sons.

But it was now the Day of Atonement. Genuine fear,
dread, deep reverence, and perhaps even some bitterness
at the loss of his sons possessed Aaron as he parted
the curtains and stood behind the gold-covered Ark and
Mercy Seat, above which was the glory of God.

The crowd waiting outside the tabernacle on the Day of
Atonement knew Aaron and the tragedy that had
marked his life. If human nature was as skeptical then as
it is now, no doubt some of those in the crowd might
have wished for someone with a better record of success
to be inside the tabernacle at that moment.

The people knew the importance of this occasion. It
was a solemn feast, one to be accompanied by a mood
of sorrow for sin. The occasion was intended to make
them individually and corporately aware of their sinfulness.
The High Priest, chosen from among them and made
clean through many ceremonial washings and anointings,
would, the people hoped, meet God's requirement in
approaching his throne on the people's behalf.

And who was being sent in that day? The man who
had led them astray, the man whose sons, Nadab and
Abihu, had followed Aaron's example and had died.
But Aaron lived and continued as High Priest. Surely
someone more worthy than he could have been found,
some of the waiting people must have thought.

# FOUR
# **FAILURE**

I used to think that most of the bad sins we commit, the ones that cause others to suffer, are made with great deliberation, after long periods of straying from God. I never wanted to believe that a Christian could fall far in a short time. Somehow I thought there was some safety in gradualism. Apparently Aaron did too.

I didn't deliberately set out to disobey God. I thought my faith stood quite firm. Years of ministry in several small churches, missionary service, working with students, and many one-to-one discipleship opportunities must have lulled me to a dangerous point of overconfidence.

Relationships with the opposite sex had never been a problem. On several occasions, when it might have been easy to give in to temptation, the moment had come and gone without a failure. In fact, I'd come through all of these temptations with a renewed sense of dedication to avoid even the opportunity of temptation and the risk of a lost reputation.

Aaron and his failure had been an enigma to me, but from the moment I took Aaron's way out by giving in to the pressure of others, his story was no longer hard to understand.

When I allowed the woman I was trying to help to visit me alone in my office and to call me at arranged times, it went against what I knew was wise, and in doing so, I was no better than Aaron. To take the wrong means to help others, as I thought I was doing, even when my motives were initially good, was to commit the sin of Aaron. In trying to do things my way, I became entrapped in an emotional involvement.

Both Aaron and I are examples of overstepping the boundaries God has set. Aaron should have said, "Moses will be back and that's good enough for me," but instead he decided that it was time for him to act. After all, he must have rationalized, he was the only leader left. Somebody had to do something. He had acted before and God had always been behind him. Why not this time too? Why not? Because to do so was overstepping. And God wouldn't bless that—then nor now.

For years I had been extremely careful about women. But in that unguarded moment, like Aaron, I decided that a good track record of success in dealing with human relations made me exempt from failure. With such an attitude, I foolishly overlooked the safeguards that should have been placed around such a relationship.

When several friends questioned me about what was happening, I reacted angrily. How much help had other people been in solving this woman's problems? Their "normal" reactions to her had driven her farther from the answers, I said. I thought, "People are more concerned about kicking someone who is down than they are about the downed person's recovery."

At first the people who questioned me were wrong about me. But then I almost quit caring what people thought and chose to do what I thought was right, no matter how it appeared.

"Aaron, oh, Aaron, why couldn't you have waited longer?" I asked that question of myself, with my name replacing Aaron's many times in the months that followed.

Because of the amount of time I spent with this woman it soon became clear to those who knew both of us just how much she had come to mean to me. I loudly denied it, largely because I didn't want to admit it even to myself. When a tormenting conscience finally won through and I faced what was really happening, the relationship was broken off, deep depression set in, and at once my world started to come apart as friends and family, who had a right to expect better things of me, believed that the very worst had happened.

I can, in retrospect, think of dozens of reasons why I should have taken another direction in trying to help this woman friend who was in marital trouble. I kept hearing the woman say that she wanted out, that she felt rejected by her husband and family. I didn't want anything I did to be interpreted as yet another rejection for her to feel. I thought that through me God wanted to show this woman his love and acceptance despite what her past failures had been. I realize now that God had no part in my losing control of my own emotions.

In sympathizing with this woman's feelings of rejection, I awakened some of my own old psychological needs, unwarranted feelings that I myself wasn't really loved either. The truth finally dawned that I was trying to fill a neurotic need for love with someone who had as many neurotic needs herself. Like many others in such a low state of mind, I allowed myself to go against all that I knew was right about such a relationship. Like Aaron, I simply overstepped.

Aaron built a golden calf, and immediately Moses was instructed to leave the mountain where he was communing with God and return to set the camp in order. The calf was destroyed and the people were punished severely.

Aaron's shame must have gone deep, enough for him to look for any conceivable alibi for what he had done. Who would have believed his story: "I threw it (the gold) into the fire, and out came this calf!" Just pure accident—presto! From a pile of gold trinkets suddenly comes a graven golden image!

However good Aaron's intentions had been, it brought little comfort to him as God's judgment began to fall on the people. The difference between wanting to do well and doing well is often a fine line, sometimes almost imperceptible. Doing what God has told us to do and doing what we think God might want us to do, even what seems to be the right thing to do at the moment, are poles apart.

How subtly closes the trap set by the evil one who uses even our good motives to make us take the wrong way. Wave after wave of apparently good intentions can dissipate the best of human efforts. Our human frame of reference has often allowed us to substitute what we think is good for what God really wants us to do. Human efforts, for which we pour out our lives for whatever altruistic motive, are the type of sin which Aaron committed, the substitution of human judgment about what we think is right for what God says is right.

Aaron didn't deliberately set aside God's wisdom for his own. His sin was rather an act of expediency, an attempt to solve a situation in a manner befitting a leader to whom the multitude was looking for answers: "Moses is gone, we don't know where he is. Something has to be done. You're a leader; do something!" Aaron's solution was to get the people busy thinking about God by any means available. A golden calf might do it, he thought.

I had no answers either when I thought the time had come for action. I only knew what I saw in this woman: anger, depression, pain, bewilderment, and despair. Bouncing from one unsatisfactory solution to another, my distraught friend, looking for someone to listen to her, unburdened to me. She needed answers. She seemed so

far out of touch with the Lord that she couldn't seem
to hear from him directly. She thought I might hear him
for her and relay the message.

Many nights I lay awake in prayer for her and for
others I knew who needed to hear from heaven. And I
prayed for myself. I too was discouraged and hurting
because I didn't have answers. Not only could I not find
help for her, I was having trouble finding answers for
myself. My distraught friend needed to know a new sense
of God's love, and perhaps she unfairly expected to
find it in me.

The more I tried to help her, the more overwhelmed I
became in my own neurotic and unfounded feelings
of being unloved. Until she came along, I had such feelings
under control.

Two people with such an emotional need are obviously
incapable of properly meeting each other's needs. I
realize now that in such a situation each one awakens in
the other the yearnings for fulfillment that only one's
mate is legitimately allowed to fulfill.

Like many others, this woman was so angry and hurt
from feeling neglected and unloved that she had given
up the idea of trying to rebuild the strained and broken
relationship with her husband. And she thought she
had found in me all that she felt she was missing in her
marriage.

When a man and a woman meet, a chain reaction can
be set off that, when legitimate, can become one of
the highest experiences in life. But when it is illicit, it
becomes one of life's lowest and most painful times.

Because physical attraction of the sexes is such a
powerful feeling and such a dynamic force within
us, it needs control—which is one of the gifts God gave
to us. Nothing is more right and beautiful than sexual
attraction in the right context of time and place, and
nothing is so wrong and ugly in the wrong time and
place.

Many earnest people naively think that a sexual attraction is always the culprit when the wrong kind of love relationship develops. "She dressed too seductively," or, "He was too suggestive with his talk," they say. They may be correct in many cases, but often the physical part was not the beginning of such a relationship but the culmination, the climax, the pinnacle experience.

As Aaron and his people were looking for immediate answers from God, they pushed each other to disobedience. They did it by their own impatience, expecting answers from Aaron. And Aaron did it by his pride, in thinking that as a leader it was incumbent upon him to act for God.

Pastors and marriage counselors who try to pick up the pieces of broken lives tell us a variety of things about why such people fall in love with each other.

"She was the only person who really listened to me. I was important to her," the man often says, implying that his wife wasn't a good listener nor a person who affirmed him. "He was a very caring person. He was really interested in me as a person. I was able to tell him things about myself that I never told anyone else before—not even my parents, or my pastor, even my very best girl friend, and certainly not my husband," she says, implying that her husband didn't know how to listen to her.

When an intimate relationship begins, no matter who the people are, both parties feel perfectly safe in sharing any information or feelings with the other, knowing that he or she will be accepted.

An intimacy formed outside marriage implies that in the former, or proper, relationship with the person's own mate, such feelings of safety and caring don't exist, or at least, if they did exist, they were never developed or tested.

Once such an emotional intimacy is formed between two people, it becomes a golden thread holding their lives together. Every other relationship grows pale and meaningless in its dazzling light.

Such an emotional attraction, far more satisfying than even physical love, is very, very powerful. It is this that draws people into the strongest bonds people can know. It is the kind of loving, caring friendship that should seal every marriage. Such a relationship is rarely shaken apart by a third party. But a marriage that doesn't have that kind of intimacy, that ability or willingness to share completely with one's mate, is much more likely to crumble if someone appears to offer the unhappy partner what he or she thinks is missing. A woman or man who feels unloved and unneeded falls easy prey to someone who appears with love, sympathy, and soft words. The attraction is even greater when such a person bares his or her own soul to feelings of not being loved nor needed. As mutual compassion pours forth, the golden thread of loving, caring intimacy is joined.

First it is information they share, then opinions, then feelings, mutual concerns, love, understanding. Soon, if they continue, nothing is held back, not even the ultimate expression of love.

It would be bad enough if such a sad episode of the grief-stricken woman occurred only once in human history. But the world is old now, and this story has told itself many times by many people who loved, and lost, and wept alone in anger and remorse when it was over. A woman and her employer, a pastor and one of his church members, a teacher and someone in his or her class. No vocation or profession is immune. The pair may be neighbors, friends, classmates. They meet, they admire, they talk, laugh, and then they fall in love. Then they cry when the affection they develop for each other has to be given up. Sometimes they hang on and selfishly destroy other loved ones, their homes, their children.

When an intimacy begins, all human frailties in the

other person are totally overlooked. The obvious becomes invisible; both feel suddenly more alive than ever in their lives. When heaven can bless an intimacy, God showers joy on the participants which mirrors heaven itself. Certainly this is how God loves us in Christ, and such love reflects his intimate, loving, caring relationship to his church.

An intimate love relationship can become so strong that the lovers see only each other. Sometimes they even become oblivious to what God may think of it and they may neglect responsibilities that God has given them. Men and women who have walked circumspectly all their lives suddenly are willing to cast aside jobs, homes, reputations, children, friends, even their spiritual integrity, to foster that one relationship which for the moment has become more important than life itself.

# FIVE
# CORRECTED AND LOVED

John Mark must have shown some promise to have been asked to accompany Paul and Barnabas on their first missionary journey into Asia Minor. But before the journey got well under way, the going got too rough for John Mark, and he decided to return home. Paul was disappointed at Mark's decision. John Mark's Uncle Barnabas was probably embarrassed at the young man's failure. Bringing John Mark along may have been his idea.

A year or so later Paul and Barnabas were preparing another missionary trip, and the question came up about John Mark's accompanying them again. There was a sharp exchange of words between Paul and Barnabas. Paul said there was no proof that Mark wouldn't fail the second time. Barnabas thought John Mark needed to be given another chance to prove himself.

We shouldn't be surprised that two fine Christian men like Paul and Barnabas should disagree over that issue. The same kind of issues come up every day in churches around the world.

For example, a man holds a responsible position in a Christian organization. He struggles with an unhappy marriage and yet tries to maintain a ministry to others.

One day it becomes clear that a divorce is imminent and yet people around him don't feel he did everything he could to repair his shaky marriage. Should the man be allowed to continue in a place of responsibility or should others be considered for the promotion due him?

In another situation, a husband ignores his wife's emotional needs for years and years. Finally in desperation his wife becomes involved with another man. The husband realizes his failure to be sensitive to her needs and wants another chance to be the kind of husband he should have been. Instead of accepting his attempts at reconciliation, the wife is so filled with resentment and anger that she takes no pleasure in the sudden outpouring of gifts and affection.

A wife begins to feel neglected by a husband who has allowed his job to be his mistress for years. In her frustrated state she is seduced by a family friend. Unable to handle the guilt, she confesses to her husband. The questions arise: How do I know she won't do it again? Can I really forgive her and forget it?

A young person gets caught up with the crowd and commits a serious crime. Parents and judges must answer the question: Did he know what he was doing? Does he really deserve another chance? Has he learned his lesson?

Satan's tactics from the beginning have been to make us ignore the important truth that sin has its consequences—if not now, then in the future. God said that Adam and Eve would die if they ate of the tree of the knowledge of good and evil. Satan immediately appeared to tell them that the results wouldn't be deadly but that the fruit would make them as wise as God.

Satan's lie was a typical half-truth. By eating the forbidden fruit, they did become aware of certain facts that God had purposely withheld from them. They didn't fall over dead immediately, but they did experience spiritual death—separation from the life and blessing of God.

John Mark may have thought that because he was young, or was related to Barnabas, his failure would be excused, that his fainthearted retreat from duty wouldn't have consequences. But he learned the hard way that it did. The Apostle Paul lost confidence in him. Being rejected as a traveling companion must have been an embarrassing put-down for the young man.

Someone who does some important work, who holds a critical job in a Christian organization, may think his problem can be overlooked because of who he is. Unhappiness can be a heavy burden to bear when the happiness and warmth provided by some woman friend is so readily available. Loneliness and the feeling of not being loved can be a terrible enticement to self-pity and self-indulgence. Common sense usually goes out the window when the opportunity to give and receive affection knocks at the door of a person who feels unloved. In the rush of emotional fulfillment the consequences of sin can be easily ignored as many Christian leaders have discovered.

The words of a song, popular for a number of years, reflect with devastating honesty the sentiment of many people today: "If lovin' you is wrong, I don't wanna be right." It is not hard to understand how Satan can use this powerful human emotional drive, the need to be loved, to bring down so many people. Just as the Duke of Windsor gave up the throne of England to marry the woman he loved, many hundreds of Christian men and women have been tempted to throw away a reputation, a ministry, even their standing with the Lord for something or someone they love!

But what an arbitrary, disorderly world it would be if sin had no consequences! For John Mark the consequences of his failure were the displeasure of Paul and the loss of responsibility and respect. For the Christian worker, it is the displeasure of his employers and the threat of losing his job.

The man who neglects his wife could say that his long hours on the job are really for her sake, to buy her all the things she wants. Or he could say she isn't meeting his needs, forcing him to withdraw into his work as an escape from his own unhappiness. But the sin of neglecting his mate has its consequences. His wife's patience runs out.

Perhaps her threat to leave him isn't the best way to get his attention, but some marriages never seem to get better until one of them says, "I've had enough; unless something changes, I want out."

Sin has its consequences. A broken marriage and the loss of a mate are sometimes the price people pay for the sin of mistreatment and neglect.

The woman who allows herself to be seduced because she feels lonely and unloved faces serious consequences for her sin. She risks losing her husband, her family, her reputation—everything of real value. The fear of sin's consequences operates in the Christian's soul as the fear of physical pain does in the physical body. Without pain to warn us of physical harm, we would destroy our bodies very quickly. In the same way, if we faced no earthly consequences for sin, our souls would soon drift into spiritual disuse and neglect.

Life has its earthly as well as its eternal rewards and consequences. Yet it is clear that God allows things to happen to discipline us, to keep us away from sin and to reward us for obedience.

Thank God for Paul, who stood firm against John Mark. If he hadn't, Mark and millions after him would have been tempted to carelessness about spiritual commitment. And thank God for churches and organizations that hold their standards high, who hold people responsible for their behavior, to keep people on their toes spiritually. Obviously, the censure of some Christians is part of the discipline God puts in our lives to shape us for effective service.

I became a Christian during my senior year of high school. For nearly a year after my conversion I struggled to overcome the habit of smoking. I finally got off cigarettes but then, foolishly, two years later I started smoking again. I was in the Army then, and one cold night while on guard duty, I lit up to keep warm. I knew the moment that I took the first puff that I was entrapped again by the habit.

Two years later I enrolled in a small Christian college where smoking was forbidden. Almost every day for several months I sneaked off into town for a smoke. I fought the habit for quite a while, smoking in service station restrooms all around town and at home during weekends off campus.

One day my roommate, who could smell the cigarette smoke on my breath, forced the issue. He told me that either I was to tell the dean of men or he was going to. He gave me twenty-four hours to think about it.

I knew he was serious, so I decided to be the one to tell the dean. I made an appointment with the dean's secretary and spent a sleepless night worrying about what I was going to say the next morning. I fully expected to be told to pack up and go home.

All night I thought about the many people who would be disappointed at my failure to stick it out at Bible college. Most of all, I wondered why I hadn't been able to appropriate God's power to overcome the habit. Was this the beginning of many more failures for me? What was going to become of me? I really felt rotten, defeated, discouraged, depressed, but mostly angry with myself, and ready to give up. In some ways, I felt as John Mark must have felt, listening to Paul and Barnabas discuss his failures.

Next morning I nervously sat down in front of the dean's desk and unfolded my story.

"Well, Wight, do you think smoking is wrong?" I wasn't prepared for such a question. That was 1954, years before medical research had discovered the strong relationship between cigarette smoking and diseases of the heart and lungs.

"I knew the school rules, so for me it was wrong," I answered.

"That wasn't my question," he countered. "As far as I'm concerned, by your coming in this morning to tell me about it you've made that part of it right, as much as you can. I'm asking you if you think it's morally wrong to smoke."

I really didn't know. Growing up in the South, I had known many people, even pastors, who had smoked all their lives.

The dean gave me several books to take along to study, told me to come back to see him every other day for a while to give him a report on whether or not I had done anything about the habit.

Before I left, he offered a long, tender, caring prayer for me. Whatever wrong I had done, with his big hand on my shoulder I felt I was being forgiven. No longer an enemy, he was a friend who was going to stand with me in my problem until we had seen it through.

It was as if new life was pouring through his fingers into me. I knew nothing magical was happening. It was simply an experience of the power of forgiveness, an act of love that awakened within a defeated person the desire to try again. It was the good news of a second chance.

I have since told many people around the country that I feel I owe my whole Christian experience to that loving man who gave me a second chance. I know God would have been able to meet me at some other time and perhaps he would have used other means to bring me back to himself had this man not done so. But humanly speaking, I wonder what would have happened to me if I had left Bible college that day as defeated as I was.

We must use our imaginations to feel what John Mark was going through when he got the news that Paul wasn't going to let him go along with them on the second missionary journey. It may have taken that kind of shock to wake him up to the seriousness of his failure.

Paul was determined to be tough-minded. Barnabas had put up a good argument, but Paul held his ground. John Mark had failed, and as far as Paul was concerned, he wasn't ready for a second chance.

Why wasn't Barnabas ready to accept Paul's decision as final? We may have to wait until eternity to learn what he was thinking, but I would like to believe that he had John Mark's future in mind. So Barnabas planned a trip of his own and took John Mark with him, leaving Paul to go with Silas. For Barnabas to allow John Mark to slink away in defeat might have been the end of the young man's missionary work.

Again, we know God could have used other means to reinstate him, but humanly speaking, it would have taken quite a comeback effort. When others give up on a person who fails, it is easy for the person to give up on himself. John Mark had not only failure to overcome but discouragement as well.

Thank God for a Barnabas. Until a person has lived through the shameful and bitter feelings of a lost reputation, it is hard to understand how important it is to find someone who still believes in him.

We could unfairly criticize Paul, saying he had been fortunate all his life, that he had never known failure so he couldn't possibly have understood how John Mark felt. The same unfair criticism is leveled today, an argument that seems to say that a person has to have sinned greatly before he can minister to other sinners. Those who would say *that* evidently have never identified with Paul's own confession of being "the chief of sinners." One who really doesn't sympathize with the plight of sinners understands very little of God's grace in forgiving sin.

It would be nice if all Christians could endure ill treatment like the Apostle Paul and not get bitter. Very few people ever faced such opposition. Several times he was jailed, often beaten, falsely accused. There were other hardships—several times shipwrecked, often ill—and yet we see no trace of bitterness.

Before his conversion, Paul seemed to be constantly on the rise. His academic advancement, his reputation, the responsibility given him were really phenomenal. If he ever failed seriously along the way in his rise to prominence, the Scriptures don't tell about it.

After his conversion he spent years in obscurity before his reputation as a leader in the new church came to light. The Scriptures tell of the opposition to his message and of the many things he suffered for Christ. The church leaders often challenged his teachings, but if he ever knew personal bitterness or spiritual defeat because of his sins, we don't know about it. He even went through sufferings and persecutions as a winner. Too bad we aren't all more like him!

Most of us lack the spiritual poise and stamina of Paul. We probably feel more kinship with young John Mark, who seemed to get a good start in life but soon found himself in grave defeat.

What does it take for a man like John Mark to get going again? It takes a Barnabas. His very name means "the son of exhortation" or "the son of consolation."

One of the gifts of the Spirit mentioned in Romans 12 is the gift of exhortation, *paraklesis*, the same word used of Barnabas and of the Holy Spirit.

The ministry of *paraklesis* is twofold. It involves both
exhortation and comfort or consolation. How one-sided
would be the ministry of the Holy Spirit if he only
comforted us! When we are behaving badly he comes to
bring conviction and to turn us from our sins.

How inadequate would be one who exercises the gift
of exhortation if all his messages to the church were
hell-fire and brimstone and never words of comfort and
encouragement when comfort was needed!

Barnabas served an important purpose in John Mark's
life. Barnabas seemed to be a New Testament example
of the gift of exhortation. His ministry translated to John
Mark in very personal and practical terms.

Barnabas must have made certain that Mark knew how
serious his failure had been. The Holy Spirit hardly
brings about changes in the life of a person who is satisfied
with the status quo. Like my former dean of men,
Barnabas understood that someone has to forgive one
who is a failure so that he can start forgiving himself and
start working toward better results. For Barnabas to
take Mark along with him must have been an important
step in the young man's recovery.

And for John Mark, the ministry of exhortation and
consolation offered him by the Holy Spirit through Barnabas
demanded a response. He could either give up and go
back home again for good or he could accept Barnabas'
offer and begin working on his recovery.

John Mark had to admit his failure and he had to
accept Paul's criticism before he was really prepared to
receive the mercy offered by Barnabas. Sins not repented
of are sins not forsaken or forgiven. In the same way,
before I ever got rid of the smoking habit, I had to be
convinced that it was wrong and displeasing to God.

John Mark had to accept the forgiveness offered him.
The act of going with Barnabas, and this time doing
an acceptable job, was proof of his desire to put his past
behind him. Some people at this point never recover

because they are too proud to admit that they have done anything that needs forgiveness. The only thing worse than failure is hanging on to the false pride that keeps the person in defeat.

John Mark also had to forgive himself. Often a big part of feeling forgiven is the return of self-respect. Nothing restores self-esteem like being forgiven by others coupled with a taste of success in the place where failure had been experienced. The two go together.

I will never forget those agonizing hours in Bible college, sitting in class, trying to keep my eyes on the Lord, and trying to keep my word to the dean of men, while all the while churning inside for another smoke. All that kept me going during those days was the encouraging smile of the dean each time I reported another milepost of success, three days without a cigarette, then two weeks, finally two whole months without a smoke! I felt so good that once the physical craving was driven from my system I never desired to smoke again.

Recognizing the importance of success, John Mark knew that he needed to discipline himself lest another opportunity for service slip away. He had to get back to work.

For me, one of the most heartwarming passages in the Bible is Paul's words written to Timothy: "Get Mark and bring him with you, because he is helpful to me in the ministry" (2 Tim. 4:11). Paul, the one who turned down John Mark because he had failed, is now asking for Mark to be at his side because the young man had proven himself useful. These words sound like a full recovery for someone who once looked like a lost cause. The recovery had taken place partly because somebody stood by him and helped him to recover.

The old question comes to us: Who was right in that controversy between Paul and Barnabas? I believe that both were right. Paul was right to demand high standards. A sluggard needs exhortation to make him wake up to the seriousness of life. But Barnabas was right also. Someone needed to show mercy and offer Mark another chance. After all, how can failure ever turn to success without an opportunity to try again?

When parents are in disagreement about the discipline of their children it is sometimes because one of them wants to discipline the child severely at a time when the other parent wants to show love and mercy. Parents, we are rightly told, should agree at such times. Yet I can remember times when my father was doling out harsh punishment and I never questioned the fact that he was right in trying to turn me away from some of the things I was doing. On many such occasions my mother would plead for leniency to show the other side of discipline, which is love and forgiveness. I never once lost respect for her or thought she was too weak. I don't think I loved or respected one of them more than the other for their temporary or apparent unevenness toward me. I realize now that I needed to see both sides of parenting—the high standards being expected and the love and forgiveness when I didn't always deserve it.

The story of Paul, Barnabas, and John Mark teaches us an important truth about the Christian church. We need each other. We need the ministry that many people can give us. Sometimes we need the figurative kick in the pants that some member can give us—the exhortation, the rebuke. Other times we need a kiss on the forehead from someone else—the comfort, the consolation.

Some people try to solve all their own problems alone with God. If they really can do it, they will probably find better, more lasting results and greater dependency upon God. But other people who really need help don't seem to know how to find that help or don't fully realize their need for it. God often leads others to seek them out, to exhort them, to comfort and console them, to bring them to spiritual health. We need to be sensitive to the Spirit's leading so that we don't unnecessarily intrude into another's personal affairs with improper motives. Nor do we want to comfort someone whom God is bringing to conviction. Sometimes people really can't work out their own problems by themselves. That is why God sends along other people like Barnabas. Discouraged, defeated people especially need them. Thank God for "sons of consolation" like Barnabas.

More than ten years had passed since that morning I turned myself in at the dean's office. By that time I was a missionary home on furlough from Africa. I had taken off several weeks from visiting and speaking in supporting churches to accompany the choir of the Bible college on their summer tour, serving as their choir chaplain. It had been an exciting two weeks filled with many spiritual victories, both in the congregations where we ministered and in the lives of student choir members. I had prayed and counseled with many of them along the way, and had daily ministered to them from the Bible.

As the bus arrived back on campus at the end of the tour, the first person I saw as I walked through the administration building was John Kerr Munro, the dean of men who had seen me through my time of failure during my freshman year. He was then director of admissions for the school.

I walked up to him, took his hand, and tried to talk to him. But I couldn't—I became so filled up emotionally that my throat cramped and my eyes poured tears so that I could hardly see. I was overwhelmed again with gratitude to my old friend, my faithful Barnabas, the man who had brought both conviction and comfort to me at a difficult time in my life.

Later it dawned on me just what Bible passages I had used for the devotional studies with the choir during

the tour, studies that had brought so much blessing to me
and to the students. We had studied the Gospel of
Mark, the book written by the man who had recovered
from being a dismal failure, the man who had been
given a second chance.

Then it occurred to me that I might never have been
on that tour to teach from Mark's Gospel had not another
Barnabas also given me a second chance.

I will never know if my friend John Munro foresaw
such a day. But I will always be glad that he got to see
that taking a chance with me had been worth it. At a
time when I thought I was losing something precious that
God had given to me, John Munro gave back to me a
sense of usefulness and my joy in Christ. Often as
I'm praying, asking God to make me more Christlike, I
ask him to make me like John Kerr Munro, and like
Barnabas.

Now, as I thought of what Barnabas was to John Mark,
and what John Munro had been to me so many years
ago, I knew I needed help again. I needed encouragement,
forgiveness. But would that help come?

For months I was too ashamed to think about the poor
reputation I had acquired. When the crisis came and
went, I did everything I knew to make right all that had
gone wrong and to correct the wrong. Realizing my
own family relationship was in jeopardy and eager to get
the help I needed, I started going for counseling to a
number of Christian friends as well as professionals. God
began to work some healthy changes in my life during
those days. Hard decisions to start making some right
choices, no matter how I felt, did eventually bring
about the healing I needed. But it was painful and it took
a long time.

# Discouraged Servant
## (1 Kings 19)

Elijah sensed that he could still feel the heat of Jezebel's anger across the miles to where he had hidden himself. Frustrated and tired, he slumped in the shade of a gnarled broom tree. At that same moment Jezebel's soldiers were trying to find him to kill him. Yet it wasn't because of Jezebel's anger that he fled; it was because of his own.

Every dropping twig jerked him to his feet with a start. He was discouraged enough to die, yet he fled Jezebel, choosing death by starvation in the desert at the hand of God rather than death by the swords of Jezebel's henchmen.

The last two days had changed the course of his life—perhaps of the entire nation of Israel. The crisis he had precipitated the day before on Mount Carmel would make it impossible for anything to be the same ever again. Jezebel's priests of Baal had been slain. For that she would never forgive him. Obviously God's miracle hadn't changed her heart in any way; it was even harder.

There was no reasonable explanation for her pursuing him, nor was there an explanation for his running from her. He should have been riding the crest of glory instead of hiding like a jackal in the wilderness, fearing for his life.

Yesterday the fire of God had fallen at his bidding, as
had the long-sought rains. Judgment had fallen on Jezebel's
prophets of Baal. He had hoped their death would put
an end to Baal worship, this growing cancer on Israel's
spiritual life. But nothing had changed. No ground
swell of the people to overthrow the idolatrous king and
queen took place. Now Jezebel, enraged at the death
of her host of prophets, rather than being subdued, was
all the more set on destroying Elijah and the message
from Jehovah.

From the story in Scripture it appears that Elijah could
have been slain already had Jezebel chosen. The
messenger who brought the threat against him could have
carried instead a sword to slay him. But her threat
could possibly solve her problem just as well. If she could
force him into silence or seclusion or make him flee
the land, it would relieve her of having to risk God's
wrath upon herself for slaying him.

Whether from fear of her threats or discouragement
about the failure of his mission on Mount Carmel, Elijah
chose to flee.

Lying under the broom tree, the prophet was fighting a
battle in his heart, a trial greater than the one just
concluded on Mount Carmel and the contest with the
prophets of Baal. Lips that yesterday had called down fire
from the Lord were today asking God to take his life.
"I've had enough, Lord," he said. "Take my life. I am no
better than my ancestors."

His courage, sense of purpose, and all desire seemed
to have gone, just as the smoke of the sacrificial animals
had on Mount Carmel the day before. The prophet
had tried, and even with the dramatic show of God's
power on his behalf, his mission seemed ultimately
to have failed. The people would soon forget the display.
It was all for nothing. Jezebel would get her way after
all. Another horde of priests of Baal would rise like weeds

to replace the ones that had been slain. "I might as well be dead," he thought. Heaven-sent sleep finally silenced the weary champion. Elijah might as well sleep. He had done all he could. The next step was God's. The One who spoke in thunder and fire on Mount Carmel had not finished speaking nor working for his physically and emotionally spent servant. While Elijah slept, the answer was already on the way.

"Then he lay under the tree and fell asleep. And at once an angel touched him and said, 'Get up and eat.' He looked up and there by his head was a cake of bread baked over hot coals, and a jar of water. He ate and drank and then lay down again" (1 Kings 19:5, 6).

Again the angel awakened him. "The angel of the Lord came back a second time and touched him and said, 'Get up and eat, for the journey is too much for you.' So he got up and ate and drank. Strengthened by that food, he traveled forty days and nights until he reached Horeb, the mount of God. There he went into a cave and spent the night" (vv. 8, 9).

Many years earlier God had provided for his servants in Canaan, the place God had promised to bless. But now a disobedient nation, cowering before an idolatrous king and queen, had failed to trust in Jehovah when Elijah, their second Moses, brought down the fire of God on the mountain. This time the steps seemed reversed. Elijah spent not forty years, but forty days of wandering in the wilderness, going south to Horeb, the mountain of God. He seemed to be retreating vicariously for all the people of God, going back to the place where God had claimed Israel as his own. It was as if Elijah was seeking a new start and a new direction—at least a new message.

The distance from Jezreel to Horeb is fewer than two hundred miles. It could have been trekked in fewer than ten days. But perhaps it may have taken the forty days of wilderness walking for God's prophet to relearn the truth that the miraculous provision of God is adequate sustenance for all of life's pilgrimage.

The Bible isn't clear as to Elijah's direction. The angel said his journey would be long, but we really don't know who or what directed Elijah to go to Mount Horeb. Perhaps it was Elijah's way of finding out if God really was done with him.

People who have never been depressed enough to wish themselves dead, as Elijah did, have difficulty understanding this kind of behavior. If Elijah really wanted to die, he could easily have returned to Jezebel and she would have accommodated him. But such an act would have been inconsistent with his trust in God.

Elijah's anguish was a result of the apparent failure of his mission. Death was to come as his final act of grief to be rendered up for God alone to see and feel. If death should come, it must be there in the desert where God through natural forces could either slay or preserve him.

But Elijah lived. He learned the truth others have learned—that angels walk through our forty days or forty years of wilderness journeys. Angels walked with trusting Israel through forty years. And angels walked with Jesus, who struggled forty days with Satan.

When the prophet reached Horeb, he looked for God to be there to speak again from his holy mountain. Elijah sat in the cave, his pride gone, perhaps most of his anger as well. Subdued, humbled, mellowed, the prophet settled down to wait. Then a voice stirred him. A forty-day silence was broken. "What are you doing here, Elijah?"

"I have been very zealous for the Lord Almighty," Elijah replied. "The Israelites have rejected your covenant, broken down your altars, and put your prophets to death with the sword. I am the only one left, and now they are trying to kill me" (v. 14).

That was reason enough for Elijah to be discouraged, to be running, to be depressed, he thought. But that was because he was reckoning only on what he heard and saw. Despite the Mount Carmel demonstration and the miraculous feeding by the angel, Elijah was still missing the point.

*The Lord said, "Go out and stand on the mountain in the presence of the Lord, for the Lord is about to pass by." Then a great and powerful wind tore the mountains apart and shattered the rocks before the Lord, but the Lord was not in the wind. After the wind there was an earthquake, but the Lord was not in the earthquake. After the earthquake came a fire, but the Lord was not in the fire. And after the fire came a gentle whisper. When Elijah heard it he pulled his cloak over his face and went out and stood at the mouth of the cave. Then a voice said to him, "What are you doing here, Elijah?" (vv. 11-13).*

The second time the question came it was to an awakened prophet who now understood. Just as God was not in the wind, earthquake, or fire, neither was he in the turmoil raging in Elijah's world. God spoke instead in the quieting, the stilling, the quenching of wind, earthquake, and fire.

Again Elijah answered, but this time not in accusation or blame but in quiet explanation of his own dilemma. As Moses of old, who perhaps stood in that same spot when rebellious Israel had broken the law and rejected the covenant of God, the prophet needed to know what God would do on his behalf as he stood for his covenant-breaking people. But more than that, Elijah needed to know what a dedicated servant of God was going to do when the people to whom he was trying to minister no longer wanted him.

"The Lord said to (Elijah), 'Go back the way you came, and go to . . . anoint Hazael . . . Also anoint Jehu . . . and anoint Elisha . . .' " (vv. 15, 16). No word of reproof, no threat, no probation period—just simple instructions. In effect, God was saying, "Get back to work. I've got things for you to do."

# SIX
# GOING DOWN TO THE BOTTOM

I felt I was the only soul in the world still awake. It was well past midnight. The hurting inside, worse than physical pain, had driven me from my bed and out onto the dark neighborhood streets. Long walks and long hours slumped over on quiet park benches gave little relief, because the pain from which I was trying to walk away was inside me and inescapable.

At forty-six years of age, it suddenly appeared that a successful career, my marriage, my family—everything precious to me—was about to disappear.

Long jumbled attempts at prayer, punctuated by tears, weeping until stomach muscles were sore to the touch, weren't enough to vent the pressure pounding inside me. I never thought a grown man could or should cry so much. Desperately I watched an emotional breakdown edging closer and closer.

All night, as I strolled the neighborhood, I kept thinking of the last seven or eight years, the happiest and by far the most fruitful, fulfilling years of my life. Even ten years on the mission field prior to that didn't compare with what the Lord had been doing in my life those past few years.

But because of what had taken place, everything that really meant anything was slipping away and I didn't know any way to get it all back. Walking the dark streets, I tried to think through all that had brought me to such a state of spiritual and emotional defeat.

A light refreshing rain began to fall. I got up from the park bench and started home, knowing that something serious had to change in my life if I was going to recover. I couldn't give up now. Something had to be done to help me profit from this anguish. Somehow this much emotional pain had to be sanctified—to be salvaged and set apart for a higher purpose, something that might help others not to fall into a similar trap.

Still, sleep didn't come for me. It was nearly daylight when I finally dozed off. Usually I would have been upset by sleeplessness, knowing I had to work the next day. But now for the first time in many years, I didn't have that kind of worry. This morning I had no job to go to.

At a time when most men with college-age children are well grooved in their careers, I was suddenly untracked, unwanted, unprofitable, and with no place to go. Priscilla and I had a little money saved, and as long as she kept working and I was able to find some free-lance projects, we would somehow stay alive until another job came along. But much more important than the money was the discouragement of having to resign from a job I really liked. Six months had passed since questions were raised about my impropriety with the woman friend I had been trying to help. My employers seemed to be genuinely trying to help me recover. But the respect I had lost from co-workers was never regained, making it impossible for me to continue. I agreed reluctantly that I ought to resign. It was painful and embarrassing to know that I was no longer needed or wanted. I had hoped my bosses would give me more time, but they pressed me for the decision.

Having lost the job would have been easier to take if I hadn't liked it so well and all the people with whom I worked. I was trying to put my failure behind me and was just beginning to feel that I was on top of the situation again. I thought I had done everything I could do to put my life back in order in my family and in my personal affairs. I was marveling at the strength that came from the Lord and from some of his servants who helped me get myself going again.

I was thankful to the Lord for the restoration he had brought to me. There had been months of solid rebuilding for my wife and me. We had many painful talks with Christian counselors and friends, trying to help me understand why I had stumbled so carelessly. I believed that it was the fiercest attack of Satan I had ever known. It had been a terrible conflict. No fire came down from God on a Mount Carmel, but I had experienced his forgiveness and what I thought was a vindicating victory. I began to think that the problem and its consequences were forever behind me. But then the bottom fell out. The decision was made with my company that it would be better for me to leave than try to stick it out. Those who believed the worst about me were not going to let the issue drop.

It was just as well. During those preceding months I had been facing a number of trying situations on the job. A reorganization within the company and my department had taken much of the interest and challenge out of my job description. Many times I had been tempted to look elsewhere for another job, but every time something within me told me to stop running and face the situation, no matter how difficult it seemed. If I had failed, it would be better to stay and find victory on the battlefield on which I had previously lost.

In spite of my unsettled state, I knew deep down that I had a calling from God. Something important had happened to me years before. On a steamy Sunday afternoon in 1959 in Atlanta, Georgia, I had met with my pastor and a group of other local ministers who examined me and ordained me to the gospel ministry. Something irrevocable took place that day, something I could not bring myself to forget. Whatever I did, I knew I couldn't step out of the Lord's work.

After the ordination service we left the church in Atlanta that night in 1959 to drive the 200 miles home in a driving rainstorm that literally forced us off the road several times. All through that storm and all the stormy, dark, distressing hours and years that followed, I knew I would never be satisfied with a job that was just a job. If my work did not involve some kind of ministry that would enable me to use the gifts I thought God had given me, I would never be satisfied.

That was a decision made twenty years earlier, even though it was a commitment hard to keep now. And at the time—in spite of how I felt, no matter what people chose to believe about me—I would have to do what I thought was right, to stay in Christian work. But why couldn't others recognize it as well? Why did doing the right thing have to hurt so much? One of the reasons I could have given for wanting to stay on the job was that I wanted the opportunity to prove myself.

That is why the message that came that dreary Thursday couldn't have been any less painful to me than was Elijah's message from Jezebel. It was time to leave, and like Elijah there was nowhere to go but to the desert.

The harsh realities of unforgiveness and misunderstanding now had their greatest impact on me. The earlier depression I had gone through was mild compared to the days and weeks that followed. Some of the bitterest feelings I had ever known welled up in my spirit. I could forgive myself for the mistakes I had made with the woman, knowing God had forgiven me. But I was learning that I couldn't expect others to be so Godlike in their forgiveness.

I was learning, like discouraged Elijah, that God's spiritual victories did not make me immune to the judgment of other people. I thought I was making a good recovery and that God was answering my prayers for help and restoration. But some of the people with whom I worked couldn't see what God was doing. Somewhat like Elijah, I was leaving in depression from the scene of what for me had been a great personal victory.

I was puzzled over those who I thought should have seen what God was doing to restore me, but who chose rather to remember other things they thought they had seen in me previously. Forgiveness doesn't come easily for some people, no matter how hard the offender may have tried to bring about reconciliation. Just as I would have to give certain people the right not to like me, I would have to allow others the right not to forgive me if that is what they chose. My responsibility before the Lord, however, remained undiminished. I would still have to pray lest the bitterness return and I start holding grudges against the people at work for their lack of forgiveness.

Many angry and fearful thoughts seized me. The knots in my stomach and tense muscles throughout my body refused to relax when I tried to sleep. The darkest thoughts came at night. My bed became a torture rack where I agonized over the disaster of the past six months that had taken me from being a useful, hard-working organization man who received compliments for his work to a disgraced, defeated, discouraged, and depressed unemployed and unemployable derelict.

The people with whom I had worked did everything as quietly as they could. They had given me the opportunity to sign a letter of resignation, so I could tell the next employer that I had left of my own choice. Like the patient before amputation surgery, I was signing the permission slip that would allow the "surgery" to be done to remove the offending limb. They would accomplish their goal over my own signature.

The evangelical Christian world seems very small sometimes. Word travels fast, like an epidemic. I had to choose my friends carefully for a while, for their sake and mine. And there were some true friends who were very Christlike in trying to uphold me in those discouraging days that followed.

I was afraid also of what this ordeal was going to do to change me. The last thing I wanted was to become a bitter, vengeful person. Self-pity and its destructive nature had already taken its toll months before. Though self-pity offers a kind of release, my giving in to it was not going to be the solution. I knew I would have to lick the depression or I wouldn't last long. I would simply have to get over the bitterness and despair. I would have to pull together all my resources, emotional and spiritual, for the task of selling myself to another employer at a time when I was already discouraged with myself. As upset as I was emotionally, enough rational thinking prevailed to convince me that the depression somehow had to go or I simply wasn't going to make it.

I knew I could look for scapegoats, people to blame because I had lost my job, but I'm sure it would have been counterproductive.

I realize now there are things more important than career success or job satisfaction—a good reputation, for instance. One career failure like the one I had experienced not only causes erosion of self-confidence, so important to spiritual recovery, but for me it negated a lot of other good credentials I had gained in the past. One might wonder if a career failure is really much different from a moral failure. Is there really such a thing as a second chance today for such failures? For me,

when I lost my job? Or for my friend, who had almost
destroyed herself with her affair?

We search the Scriptures in vain to find a scene more
tender than one of the angel feeding Elijah. Not in
green pastures, but in a desert, Elijah lay down to rest.
And even there God's angels prepared for him a feast. One
can almost see the tenderness of a loving parent, waking
a sleeping child, caring for his needs, and returning
him to his bed of slumber and security. God's child, fitfully
asleep, fearless, hardly notices the caring hands that
prepare his meal. Elijah ate his lunch and went back to
sleep.

How unlike God we are! How many a good scorching
sermon we could have preached to unbelieving Elijah
at that moment!

"What's the matter with you? Didn't you see what God
did for you yesterday? Don't you think you're acting a
bit ungrateful? Don't you know it's wrong to talk about
suicide? You should be ashamed of yourself—don't
you know suicide is a sin? Don't you see what God has
done for you in the past? Where's your faith? What
right do you have to be discouraged?"

That is what we might have said. But a loving, patient,
caring heavenly Father with no fanfare simply sends
an angel with food, wakens him, feeds him, and tucks
him in again to finish his nap. Not a word of scolding! And
with such kindness and understanding, God gives us in
this passage one of the clearest lessons about how to deal
with depressed, discouraged, burned-out servants. Food
and rest are not the only lessons we can learn from
Elijah's experience.

First, Elijah had overextended himself physically. In so
doing, he had set himself up for a fall. After the fire
had fallen and the rains had come, Elijah ran all the way
from Carmel to Jezreel, a distance of more than twenty
miles. Exhaustion after this marathon run was to be ex-

pected even though he had run it in the strength of
the Lord. Physical exhaustion is bound to affect a person,
mentally and emotionally.

Second, an emotional low often follows an emotional
high. The drama on Mount Carmel, the victory over
the prophets of Baal all in one eventful day, the miraculous
rain, and the marathon run to Jezreel were a series of
unprecedented triumphs.

Many have told of their experiences of low moods
following a holiday season or other big event such as a
concert, a graduation, a wedding, the birth of a child.
Many pastors take Monday as their day of rest so that
their low mood after Sunday's emotional high won't
involve their ministry.

Third, we should expect some of Satan's sharpest
attacks to come on the heels of some of our biggest
victories. From such attacks God never promised we
would be immune. He promised only to hear us when we
call for help, when we go back to the mountain, as
Elijah did, and wait for him to speak again.

# Living
# with the
# Consequences
## (2 Samuel 12)

Household servants stood at a distance watching, speechless with embarrassment. The once happy warrior king lay prostrate, dew-covered in the palace garden. Just months before, he had danced with jubilation as the ark of God entered Jerusalem. The one who had inspired so many to sing of joy now lay mourning in the dirt.

Twisted around his body was a wrinkled sackcloth garment, customary to someone fasting or in deep grief. Draped over his broken spirit was an even more uncomfortable shroud of his sin.

The bright scenes of the past, the triumphs over impossible enemies, were gone. Gone also were the songs he had sung to God on the hillsides near Bethlehem. Gone was the strength that had slain wild animals threatening his father's sheep. Gone were the shouts of praise from those who saw him topple mighty Goliath. The crowds, shouting praise at his victorious campaigns, were now gone. Instead, a small cluster of servants stood nearby, whispering in disgust at their fallen champion.

Inside the palace a child lay dying, and no amount of tearful remorse was going to change what God through the prophet Nathan had spoken about that child. Nathan, a faithful and courageous messenger, had brought God's piercing light into David's darkened heart to expose his sin. The child was going to die.

This sad story in the Bible is a part of Scripture we might like to remove from the record because it seems to contradict so many other truths about God's forgiveness and mercy. But the record has to be there in Scripture because the episode of the preceding chapter is also a part of the history. The death of his child, wrongly conceived, was God's response to David's sin—as the loss of Eden was God's response to Adam and Eve's sin. And it was what death in the wilderness was to unbelieving and complaining Israelites who didn't believe Moses' report of the faithful spies.

We humans are among the strangest of God's creatures. When we most need to look upward to see God, we despair and turn our eyes downward toward the dust. At such a time of deep anguish God's beloved and anointed servant David heard the whispers and knew that what he feared most had occurred. The child was dead, and further grief, however appropriate it might have felt, was now useless and unproductive. It was time to get up from the dirt.

David, dew-soaked and tear-stained, got up from the ground and entered the palace and his place of responsibility. He was the same, but different. He still loved God, perhaps more now. Never again would he appear the lighthearted hero. Through his pain he had come into the experience of just how profound God's love really was.

He returned to the same house, but to a much different household in many ways. Some things would never be the same again. The love for his family would be the same, but all his children would suffer with him from the consequences of his failures.

For years to come David would feel the consequences that were unalterably linked to his wrong acts in the past. Like a man watching a rock that he pushed down the mountain trigger a destructive landslide—however sorry, repentant, and even forgiven he may have been for what he did—he was doomed to see the destruction of the landslide take place. He would have to stand on the mountaintop and watch it happen and know that he had been responsible.

David's children might love him just as much, but could it ever be the same? Children have a way of holding their parents, sometimes unfairly, to standards much higher than they plan or hope to achieve themselves. They feel hurt and cheated when they learn that their ideals, their models, are just as human and frail as they are. As a result of what they see, they are often tempted to expect even less from themselves. The boulder and resulting landslide continue to crash downward.

David's responsibility to family and friends would be the same, yet it would be a different relationship in some ways. Before, his warm relationship with God and his integrity were examples to his family. Now, after his failure, his integrity would be shown in the way he allowed himself to recover. No longer would he be an example of God's *keeping* grace, but instead an example of God's *forgiving* and *restoring* grace.

David got up from the ground. After he had washed, put on lotions, and changed his clothes, he went into the house of the Lord and worshiped. Some serious transactions must have taken place there in those moments. The preface to Psalm 51 explains that this deeply moving Scripture record is the substance of the outpouring of David's heart before the Lord on that occasion.

He asked for mercy and forgiveness, not on the basis of his past record or his promise of reformation. He asked simply because God was by nature forgiving and longsuffering. "Have mercy on me, O God, according to your unfailing love . . . According to your great compassion blot out my transgressions" (Ps. 51:1).

David acknowledged his sin. He accepted the truth and

the seriousness of what he had done and why it had happened, which is so important to recovery. The memory of it was part of what would protect him from another such failure. "My sin is ever before me" (v. 3).

He knew nothing else could be made right until he was right with God. Restitution for sin begins with the one most offended—God. "Cleanse me with hyssop, and I will be clean" (v. 7).

He learned that emotional highs are from God—not from circumstances. There was a time when David could feel good just because he had done well and had entered into pleasant circumstances. But from the moment of his confession, his satisfaction and joy would derive from God, not as the by-product of circumstances. "Let me hear joy and gladness; let the bones you have crushed rejoice" (v. 8).

Restoration and stability were possible only through a renewed relationship with God. Usefulness to God was a gift. God would have to restore this to him. In fear, David recalled his troubled master, Saul, who floundered—helpless and useless—after the Spirit had departed from him. He feared lest he become another Saul. "Do not cast me from your presence or take your Holy Spirit from me. Restore to me the joy of your salvation, and grant me a willing spirit to sustain me" (vv. 11, 12).

Restoration would mean a new responsibility to minister to others who failed, and a renewed effort to return to effectiveness. "Then will I teach transgressors your ways, and sinners will turn back to you" (v. 13).

# SEVEN
# **DISCOVERIES**

I thought of David many nights when I was wandering the suburban streets of my neighborhood. I should have been at home those nights trying to rest instead of walking through the darkened neighborhood in rain-dampened clothes.

As with David, sleep fled from me, not because of a Nathan who had pointed his finger at me, but because my own heart was condemning me for causing innocent people to suffer on account of my failures. Like David, I had been in a place of responsibility and had allowed concerns for myself to outweigh the concerns of innocent people. Like him, instead of being a blessing, I had become a burden.

All kinds of oppressive thoughts close in when the consequences of a person's failures begin to catch up with him. Sometimes such a person tries to hide from the light of God's Word. But once the sin comes to the surface, the offender either brings his offering, his confession and repentance, or he looks for a prooftext from Scripture, or some rationalization, some excuse to justify his action, something to make the apparent wrong appear acceptable or proper in that set of circumstances.

Or the offender looks for a scapegoat, someone else
to blame for his sins.

Ultimately, like David, I would have to accept personal
responsibility for allowing myself to fail, for putting
myself in a situation so emotionally charged that I had
become confused and had allowed someone else to
become attached to me. There are more ways to offend
God than by a physical relationship, which could
easily have developed had we not brought our relationship
to an abrupt end. Accepting responsibility for sin was
the first step to relief from the guilt. I would have to say
with David, "I have sinned against the Lord," before
it might be said to me, "The Lord has taken away your
sin."

David made no excuses, and perhaps I shouldn't have
either. But my mind kept returning to another unhappy
episode in David's life. Earlier he had wanted Saul's
daughter, Michal, enough to risk his life and the lives
of his men to slay a hundred Philistines for Saul as a dowry
for Michal. There was a time when David and Michal
so delighted in each other that she also risked her own
life to help David escape from her demon-crazed father's
anger.

But at one point in David's life, Michal brought a great
sadness and anger to her husband David. As he was
ushering the ark of the covenant into Jerusalem, Michal
spoiled the day for him with an insulting remark about
his uninhibited dance of praise as he led the procession
through the streets. She accused him of vulgar behavior
and reproached him for it. The Scripture says, "Michal
despised him in her heart."

People are usually affected by criticism in direct
proportion to the importance they place on the person
making the criticism. Most of us would, of course, prefer
that everyone like us and everything that we do. But
not everyone does. When those who don't care about us

criticize us, it bothers us. But it hurts badly when we
are rejected by people we consider significant.

Seeing the men and women of Jerusalem dance with
him in the streets, singing praise to God, must have
been affirming and heartwarming for David. But the one
woman whose respect he wanted the most was sitting
on a balcony, watching him and despising him in her heart.
Evidently Michal didn't share David's love for God.

If David was like many people I know, if he was anything
like me, it would have been easier had it been the
people in the streets despising him and his wife rejoicing
with him. He could have taken the insults from others,
but not from her.

I have known people who stood up to what appeared
to be intolerable abuse from outsiders and still enjoyed
peace in their souls. They did so because they believed in
what they were doing and because someone they
regarded highly, a close friend, a parent, a soul mate, a
wife or husband, was standing with them to affirm
them, to accept them, to believe in them.

The Scriptures don't give us David's motive for his
other marriages, but it is possible that some of them were
simply to appease the rulers of the territories in which
he was staying during his flight from Saul. He married
Abigail and Bathsheba because he had not only felt a
fondness for them but because he felt he should assume
responsibility for them since he was indirectly the
reason that both of them were widows. Though his hand
had personally struck neither of their husbands, Nabal
or Uriah, he had wished them dead.

But his marriage to Michal seemed to be different. She
was his first love, the wife of his youth. Saul had given
her to another man when David fled the kingdom,
but David reclaimed her immediately on his return from
exile.

We will never know how much David was hurt when

he lost Michal's affection. Our only insight into his feelings comes from his stern reply to her and from the fact that Michal remained childless. He apparently never had relations with her again.

We could, in retrospect, say that if David and Michal's relationship had been what it should have been, he might not have been walking the rooftop that shame-filled evening when he saw Bathsheba bathing. If David had decided to look for a scapegoat, someone else to blame, he could perhaps have found it in his disrespectful wife.

In Eden, Adam told God that Eve was responsible for their disobedience in eating the forbidden fruit. Eve claimed it was the serpent's fault, the one that God himself had allowed in the garden.

Many years have passed since the day of Adam and Eve's disobedience, and David's sin, and we are still looking for someone to blame when we get into trouble. Some people blame their parents for their own bad behavior. They misunderstand the intent of the psychologists who trace the relationship of heredity and environment on personality development. The fact that our parents have an effect on our personalities doesn't give anyone a right to place the responsibility for failures on them or anyone else.

Husbands have been known to blame their wives for job failures: "She discouraged me from getting more educaton"; or, "I could have been a vice-president of the company now if my wife had been willing to move."

Wives blame husbands because the children don't turn out well: "He was never home. I had to raise them all by myself." Men blame their bosses. Children blame their teachers. Everyone seems to be looking for someone to blame for failure.

David was raised in a big family, and, no doubt, its environment affected him too. His tender personality shows through the Scripture record in many places. David

was always a man easily entreated by women, as shown
in all his encounters with them. Even this painful insult
from his wife was apparently more hurtful to him since it
came from the woman he loved. This same sensitive,
tender, emotional makeup breathes through many of his
psalms. He felt things strongly and with deep emotion, as
the youngest child in a family often does.

Such deep feelings as David had can be a blessing or a
curse. Our greatest strengths and personality traits can
provide the occasions for failure as well. The same sensitive,
emotional man who opened his heart in the psalms
was the same whose feelings went astray toward a woman
who was not legitimately his to love.

Used correctly, such temperament traits set us far
ahead in ability and usefulness, making us more sensitive
toward others and more caring. But when they are
directed toward ourselves and our own satisfaction, they
make us great abusers and misusers of God's grace.

David could have blamed Michal for his failure, saying
that her emotional abandonment left him vulnerable
to another woman. Or he could have blamed his parents
for not endowing him with a tougher, more rational
temperament. Or he could have blamed God for putting
him in a place of responsibility and giving him the
emotional temperament that could be corrupted so easily.

But that kind of scapegoat-seeking spirit isn't found
in the Scripture record. Instead we see David's self-
indictment: "I have sinned." I'm responsible—I deserve
the blame—I did it! And how we admire him for such a
confession! Even in his failure he remained a man after
God's own heart, and ours.

But in spite of his confession, the consequences of his
sin remained. The child was dying, and David was
still fasting and praying. And night was still upon him.

Perhaps the hardest part for David was going through
the dark nights. At least it was so for me. Although

no servants stood off in the distance and whispered over
my distress, I wondered, as I strolled past darkened
bedroom windows in the neighborhood, if any of those
resting there talked, as they reached for sleep, about
the grief they had read on my face when we crossed
paths at church and in the neighborhood stores. "How
much do they really know? Do they really believe the
ugly stories that are circulating?"

I couldn't be so honest and humble as David. I was
more than ready to blame my family and loved ones for
not making me feel more loved and appreciated. In
moments of destructive self-pity I reasoned that I deserved
some of the love and attention the woman I was trying
to help was ready to shower on me.

And I was angry because I wasn't happy with myself or
the personality that was so sensitive and open to hurt
from others. This temperament, whether a personality
defect passed on by my parents or a gift from God,
was partly responsible for the attraction to others and
their attraction to me.

In this situation that had caused so much pain, my
behavior had seemed a normal, spontaneous reaction.
When I first saw the woman, her face to me was an
open book—a message of pain, anguish, frustration,
depression. If others had seen what I saw, they said
nothing. At least they did nothing for her.

But when I saw her, I was too moved even to speak.
Others might say I should just have prayed and said
nothing. I felt she needed to know that Christians were
able and willing to "bear one another's burdens." Others
probably wouldn't have taken the risk, and perhaps I
shouldn't have. I didn't pry for information, knowing that
if the problem was something she could talk about,
she would. But again, I almost hated the part of me that
felt compelled to feel concern for her, to get involved.

Just a few weeks before I talked to this friend, something

had happened to make me feel the same kind of embarrassment about my feelings. Perhaps it was because I was feeling sorry for myself. I was walking through a busy parking lot, headed for my car. I came abreast of another car in which sat a woman, perhaps in her early thirties. The windows were closed and she was alone, weeping.

Our eyes met for a brief moment, and I knew I had to move on and leave her alone with her problems. I, a total stranger, had no right to stay to try to talk to her, even though I really wanted to. Even though she may have wanted me to stop, perhaps even needed to talk to someone, I thought no good could come of it; she might even misunderstand my intentions. So I went on.

When I reached my car, I found my eyes so filled with tears that I couldn't find the right key for the ignition. My hands shook so badly I couldn't have driven anyway. For several minutes I turned tears into prayers for a person I had never seen before, for a sorrow I could not name. Had she been hurt by a husband? a lover? Was she anxious about a child who was ill, or a job she had lost? I would never know. But it hurt all the same.

Part of me was ashamed and upset with myself. Was I crazy? Emotionally or psychologically unbalanced? Why couldn't I be normal? Would I have hurt for her if I weren't hurting inside for myself? Was it just a twisted kind of self-pity I was expressing?

The other part of me wanted to say, "Lord, don't ever let me become so callous that I can't feel for others when they feel pain."

Here it was happening again. This time I did take the risk. And once I shared with this woman that I was concerned enough about her to pray for her, it started a chain reaction that was hard to trace. It forged between us a friendship that went beyond its original intentions. Psychologists have names for such things. By calling what happened between us transference and counter-transference, they draw semantic circles around a set of human reactions that name, but don't solve, the problem they denote. Like medical researchers, they first name the disease and then seek its remedy.

Transference means that a person who is receiving counsel and support begins to transfer love and intimate feelings from an earlier object of love to a new object, namely the counselor. Some have thought that all counseling situations are a form of love relationship.

Countertransference describes the counselor's response as he or she returns the feelings to the one being helped. In such an emotionally involved situation, the counselor may lose objectivity and effectiveness with the one he is trying to help. The very fact that these reactions have names is evidence of how frequently they occur.

In the past, my experiences had been with younger people, mostly college students. The wider age difference between them and me made the possibility of these kinds of responses more remote. But this woman was much nearer my own age, which increased the risk of a problem. The fact that my motives were good had little effect on what happened. The emotional trap had sprung shut with my feelings on the wrong side of the fence. When I realized what had occurred, that my feelings for her had become so strong that, like her, I didn't want to let go, I broke away from the relationship and never saw her again. But rather than having helped her straighten out her emotions I had brought more confusion into her life, because I hadn't controlled my own feelings.

That was all months ago, but the man walking through suburban streets at midnight, trying to wash his con-science clean in chilling raindrops, seemed almost a stranger to me. It is not hard to understand how the human

heart could crave a place of purgatory, a place where the
defilement and pain of failure and frailty could be
washed or burned away!

After some weeks peaceful sleep once more returned to
me. From time to time moments of anger and fear
sprang up again and the feelings of helplessness, and
occasionally more self-pity. But sleep did come. Even
feelings of peace and the desire to pray returned again.

The lonely midnight streets are only a bad memory
now. Fall came early and winter was unusually cold that
year. But another springtime came, and the Lord
provided a different type of job and ministry for me. I still
cover some of the same streets late at night, but now
I'm jogging to prolong my life and to stay in good health—
not praying to die as I had done the summer before.

Accepting the guilt and the consequences was the
beginning of my recovery as it was with David. It was
time for me also to put off the sackcloth and get on with
life.

During this time, a valued friend and counselor showed
me an entirely new way of dealing with emotions. She
used a mode of therapy that goes by several names,
perhaps the most common being rational-emotive therapy.
It was enough for me to accept from her that my feelings
could be controlled by my thoughts.

She helped me to see that some of my unacceptable
behavior and attitudes were not the result of emotions but
irrational thinking. Both rational and irrational behavior
are accompanied by emotional responses. What she
showed me was as much an unlearning process as a
learning experience. I would have to unlearn all the
irrational lies I had been believing about myself so that
the unacceptable responses that accompanied them
would stop.

Some truths we feel we should always have known,
like these new concepts the counselor taught me. For me

it was an exhilarating and liberating experience to know that my problem was caused by irrational, unfounded, untrue thoughts that I had about myself, thoughts that had been ingrained through a lifetime of mishandled and misunderstood life experiences. It was an unbalanced mind or emotions that caused me to fail. The emotions were good or bad depending on the quality of the thoughts, irrational or rational, that brought on the emotions.

As David got up, washed himself, and went on with the business of being king, so I had to rise up and get on with my life. I had too many responsibilities and people depending on me to allow myself to wallow in remorse and self-pity.

Many years ago beside my bed at Bible college I had prayed, "How can you ever use me, Lord?" At the time I had been carefully studying the Scriptures, especially passages concerning the righteousness of God. I became overwhelmed with the memory of so many past sins. Coming into contact with God's Word had awakened in me what appeared to be a cesspool of unconfessed, unforgiven sins. Faced by the terrible memories, I had knelt by my bed and prayed, "Lord, how in the world could you ever use me after all I've done?" It was not mawkish sentiment. It was genuinely the worst picture of the filthiness of my sin I had ever seen. As dawn broke that morning, I was still on my knees by the bed. I began to feel there was some hope for me, but my faith was still too weak to claim the full forgiveness God had already given to me.

Now, years later, I had to put behind me a lifetime of feelings. However unloved I might have felt when I was a child or a teenager, that was no excuse to remain an emotional cripple all my life by continuing to act and feel as if I were still unloved. It is enough to know that I am loved now, divinely and unconditionally by

God, and humanly by my wife, my family, and my friends.

David comforted his wife Bathsheba. Bathsheba?
The person with whom he had so grievously sinned? Yes.
"She gave birth to a son and they named him Solomon.
The Lord loved him . . ." (2 Sam. 12:24).

Loved him? How could the Lord love the child born of
a relationship that never should have been, a relationship
founded on treachery and murder? The same way
God loves and sovereignly uses a thousand erring, failing,
repenting, worshiping, restored people every day.

Does God become less holy in accepting people like us
who have failed? I think not. Yet the sins we commit
do make even more apparent the need for a sinless
sacrifice for sin. There is a big difference between
condoning sin and forgiving sin. God never condones, or
overlooks sins. They must be paid for in order that
forgiveness may be granted.

And Christ died for our sins—all of them—so that
David and I, and you, could come back to God, so that
we may get up and wash, anoint ourselves, enter
God's house, and worship him again.

## Choosing to Do the Right Thing
### (Philemon; Colossians 3)

Sooner or later the subject was bound to come up.
Onesimus told Paul what he probably already knew:
Onesimus was a runaway slave. Somehow he had
fled his master and had gotten all the way to Rome. After
his encounter with Paul his life would never be the same.

Perhaps at one time he had shared a cell with Paul,
or had become acquainted with him through the church
which met in various homes around the city, or
remembered him as a friend of his master. Onesimus
could have gone anywhere he chose, but after he became
a believer, he decided to stay with Paul. He wanted to
minister to the needs of this dynamic man who had
introduced him to Christ. But Paul didn't agree to this.
"Onesimus, I know your master, Philemon," Paul
said. Imagine the long discussion the two of them had
about the problem! The old saint knew that if Onesimus
was not willing to fulfill his obligation to do the right
thing and return to his master, he would stay a slave
forever, no matter how far he traveled from Colosse or
Rome. A person may try to run from responsibility, but
he never really escapes it until he faces it and fulfills it.

How did Paul know that Philemon would act mercifully

if his runaway slave Onesimus returned? He didn't.
But if going back was the right thing to do, then either
Philemon would have to be merciful, or God would have
to take responsibility for the consequences. Paul must
have convinced Onesimus of that. After all, it wasn't
Philemon's anger or mercy that Onesimus had to
fear—it was God, who does not bless disobedience. God
has committed himself to the care and protection of
those who cast themselves upon him.

Paul must have been a good judge of character. He
saw developing in Onesimus the kind of character that
wanted to be useful. From Paul's words we learn that
Onesimus had been a faithful minister to him, one whom
Paul may have genuinely wanted to keep near him.

Paul may have noticed the character of Philemon when
he was in Colosse several years earlier. He knew
Philemon to be an honorable man, not likely to forget the
one who had introduced him to Christ. Paul had led
both Onesimus and Philemon to Christ, and in Paul's
eyes both men were equal before God. Both needed
God's forgiveness and grace.

Paul recognized unfinished business in the lives of both
men. Without discussing the rightness or wrongness of
slavery, Paul accepted it as a cultural and legal reality. As
Paul judged it, Philemon needed his servant back and
Onesimus needed to return to regain his integrity—even if
it meant he was returning to servitude.

If Philemon were to recognize Onesimus as more than
a servant and choose to emancipate him and treat
him as a brother in the Lord, that was his prerogative.
But Philemon was not under any legal obligation to
do so. Paul seemed to be counting on Philemon's setting
Onesimus free, but knew all the time that Philemon
might not. No one was more aware than Paul that he
might be sending his young friend back into a life of
slavery.

The Epistle to Philemon is a masterpiece of both good diplomacy and sound theology. One cannot read it without recognizing the similarity between Paul's mediation and Christ's work on our behalf in restoring us to God. Paul's appeal to Philemon was based on what he knew about the nature of God and his work in the human heart. "Yet I appeal to you on the basis of love" (Philemon 1:9), Paul wrote, appealing to Philemon's love for God and for Paul. We may search the world over for a stronger motivational force. Fear, money, prestige, all are very powerful motivators, but we know that no stronger force exists for doing the right thing than love—love for God and love for others. Paul knew it, and he was going to ask Philemon and young Onesimus to take the risk and prove it to be true in their own lives.

We know so very little about Onesimus and Philemon that we probably shouldn't conjecture too much about them. However, we might wonder what there was in the household of Philemon that made Onesimus so unhappy that he risked losing everything by fleeing as a runaway. Had Onesimus been falsely accused or mistreated? We don't know. But one thing is clear—unless Onesimus went back he would forever be a runaway.

Paul was begging: "I appeal to you for my son, Onesimus." Not for "my friend," nor for some fellow here whom he was not too sure about, but for "my son"! "I am sending him—who is my very heart—back to you. I would have liked to keep him with me so that he could take your place in helping me while I am in chains for the gospel" (vv. 12, 13).

Call it what you will—manipulation, pressure—Paul knew what every good diplomat or wrestler knows: the pressure points. How could Philemon have said "no"? He was committed to the mission to which Paul was giving his life. If Philemon could not find it in his regenerated heart to forgive and accept his runaway servant, then

Christianity and its mission had no power to accomplish
anything.

The time had come for Onesimus and Philemon to
prove the truth about redemption's work in the human
heart. If Christian love couldn't forgive and accept an
errant brother back into fellowship, then no power on earth
could bring it to pass. Paul was calling on Philemon to
prove his obedience to the words in the letter to the
Colossians, which probably arrived at the Colossian
church at the same time as the letter to Philemon. Paul
urged the believers at Colosse: "Bear with each other and
forgive whatever grievances you have against one
another. Forgive as the Lord forgave you. And over all
these virtues, put on love, which binds them all together
in perfect unity" (Col. 3:13, 14).

It was time also for Onesimus to submit to the
righteousness of God as Paul defined it to the entire church
at Colosse: "Slaves, obey your masters in everything,
and do it, not only when their eye is on you and to win
their favor, but with sincerity of heart and reverence
for the Lord" (3:22). If Onesimus couldn't submit to
Philemon, his submission to God was in question, just as
Philemon's relationship to God was in question if he
couldn't forgive and restore Onesimus.

"So if you consider me a partner, welcome him as you
would welcome me. If he has done anything wrong or
owes you anything, charge it to me . . . I will pay it back"
(vv. 17, 18). Blessed are the peacemakers!

It is hard to conceive of a deeper involvement in the
recovery and restoration of a man and his servant
than this! Only someone who understood the mediator
role of Jesus Christ could venture himself into the place
of mediator as Paul was doing.

It is God who suffers the loss of his runaways, his
prodigals. We, the runaways, all of us—too deeply involved
in our own guilt and too much in fear to return to him

who rightly claimed us—might have continued to run. And
we might have remained fugitives had not one suffered
and humbled himself in order to interpose himself between
us and God—someone who loved both the Father and
us enough to put himself in the middle as Paul was
doing.

Such a role was not forced on the Mediator. He chose
to do it. "Then I said, 'Here am I, I have come—it is
written about me in the scroll. To do your will, O my
God, is my desire' " (Ps. 40:6-8). It may cost dearly to be
a peacemaker. It cost our Peacemaker his life. But
from his death came resurrection life for a whole generation
of priests and mediators. From the darkness of a Roman
prison such a dynamic was at work reconciling human
alienation—even a runaway slave and his wealthy master
halfway across the then-known world.

His feet retraced the pathway to the house of Philemon.
Did a fellow servant meet him, take the letter from him, and
withdraw to carry it inside to master Philemon? Or did
the master and servant meet in the church assembly at
Colosse? Perhaps the pastor of the church transmitted
the letter to Philemon.

But somewhere the risk was taken. The two stood face
to face again, morally if not physically. We can almost
feel the sweaty hands of Onesimus as he tried to read the
response on the face of his master. Would he see
Philemon's eyes fill up with tears on hearing from Paul?
Or would he see the opposite reaction—a hard,
cynical, unforgiving look that said, "I've got you now!"
Which would it be?

How did Philemon respond? We simply don't know.
Something in me wants to put a happy ending to the
drama that unfolded that day in the house of Philemon.

How Philemon responded, in fact, has nothing to
do with the way we respond to our opportunities to
approach the person on the other side of our alienation,

no matter what separated member of the Body of
Christ we are called upon to forgive and accept. Without
our ever knowing if Onesimus was forgiven, perhaps
even emancipated, or if he was jailed—we know that
Onesimus did what he knew to be right by going back.

God was giving both of them another chance, and at
that moment how the one responded had nothing to
do with the other's decision. Our right and wrong choices
are not contingent on any other person's obedience,
no matter how loudly we may want to deny this truth.

We all hope that Philemon responded in forgiving love,
but we won't know until eternity. Sometimes deliverance
doesn't come. The stones fell heavily on innocent Stephen.
The axe fell heavily on the neck of Paul, the mediator
we read about in the Epistle to Philemon. Reconciliation
begins and ends in the work of Christ.

# EIGHT
# TO TRY AGAIN

I was in an office waiting room on the twentieth floor of a downtown skyscraper. Waiting in the cool, dimly lit lounge, reading the information folder of the employment counselor, I was waiting for his secretary to call me. God would have to speak to me through this man about the next step I should take. It was humiliating, knowing I must try to explain why a forty-seven-year-old man, who said he was intelligent and had excellent skills, was not already employed at some meaningful job. If God was through with me in Christian publishing, perhaps he would allow me to find a job and a purpose to keep going.

The counselor tried to sound reassuring. "I'll have you settled somewhere in no time at all," he smiled. I filled out information sheets, resumé forms, and test-answer sheets.

Back home I clipped classified ads and pedaled my bicycle to the corner mailbox every morning with big white envelopes stuffed with well-measured self-acclaim. I was trying to "sell" myself.

Week after week, there were long train rides into the city, sometimes twice a week, to discuss my situation with the employment counselor. These produced nothing. Waiting in the lounge for my appointment, I sat subdued, humbled, emotionally sterile, silent, waiting, praying.

"Lord, I have nowhere to go. I have tried every Christian organization in the area. I have followed up on every possible lead. Nothing has opened up. Perhaps it is time for me to give up the idea of Christian work."

After several months of calling Christian organizations the word was getting around that I was out of work and had been for some time. The old line, "I'm free now, and I'm a terrific asset—you can get me if you hurry," wouldn't work any more. Nothing succeeds like success, and no one looks more like a loser than someone who isn't succeeding. It became harder and harder to be enthusiastic.

What was I doing? I was doing the only thing I could do. I was waiting for an answer from some of the 75—or was it 125?—resumés I had mailed out. Yes, I was praying. But God knew how upsetting to my family a move to another city would be, and nothing was opening up in Christian work in my area, so there seemed nowhere else to go but to the secular world.

This time, as I left the counselor's office and descended in the elevator, I knew I wouldn't be back. God himself would have to speak—not with statements about how or why other people had failed me but to my situation. He would have to speak to me where I was and in spite of the storms raging in my heart each time my long white envelopes returned containing letters saying such things as:

*Thank you for your application. I have reviewed your application and find your qualifications impressive. However your experience does not match the requirements of the position as precisely as I would like.*

If that weren't painful enough, the closing paragraph

would really finish me off for the day: "We wish you every success in your career."

God would have to speak. I would just have to stand before God, the One who knew why no answers were coming, and wait. I recalled a story I had heard years before from Dr. Alan Redpath, then pastor of Moody Church in Chicago. Speaking at the Bible college I was attending, Dr. Redpath gave an illustration that has stayed in my mind, even though the rest of the sermon has long been forgotten.

As I remembered the story, one of his friends owned a hunting dog, trained to flush quail from the high grass.

On the way to the fields the first time out, they had to pass a farmer's house and barns. Waddling across the farm lot was a flock of tame geese. The dog had been trained to respond to the voice command to "stay," which meant that the dog was to stay put or keep walking his normal course until another command was given.

The dog, seeing the geese, trembled all over with desire to break and run for them.

"Stay," the owner commanded. But the young dog could not contain his eagerness. He leaped at the geese and soon the barnyard was a flurry of dog, billowing dust, and flying goose feathers.

Obviously, they didn't go hunting that day. The owner, deeply disappointed, seriously considered destroying the dog, believing that the animal was worthless for hunting if he couldn't obey commands. The owner decided to return the dog to the trainer.

The entire learning process had to be repeated. The trainer treated the animal as if he had never been in training at all. After a long, arduous process, the dog was trained again.

The owner knew what he must do. Again he started out for the same field, purposely to the same farmhouse and barns, through the same farmyard where the same flock of geese was kept. The owner knew that the dog could never be trusted unless he was taken back to the place where he had failed and there given another opportunity to succeed.

Again the geese waddled by, as enticing as before. Again the dog began to tremble, bursting with the desire to break and run at the geese again.

"Stay," the master said. "Steady! Steady!" As the man spoke, the dog turned his eyes toward his master and looked away from the geese. "Steady, steady!" On they walked, the man not allowing the dog to take his eyes off him until the two were well past the farmyard and the honking temptors.

I knew I needed that same chance to try again. I too wanted to be free from the stigma that had settled over me as a result of the crisis through which I had passed. But I still spent many remorse-filled nights thinking about the failure of the past months. One day I would think the problems of the past were behind me, that I would be able to get on with life and with my responsibilities as husband, father, and member of the working world. Then some specter from the past would rise up and remind me of my failure—a knowing look from someone who still didn't understand, or a friend confiding in me that the rumor mill was still grinding away. Then my spirits would hit bottom again.

Some of my thoughts sounded not unlike the voice of the evil one. "Everyone thinks you're a failure—no one is going to trust you again, much less forgive you! You don't need those phony people who say they forgive but prove by the way they treat you that they don't. Besides, you know what's best for you."

I thought of all the things I could do. Many of my friends worked in the secular world. If the Christian world wasn't going to use me, maybe I should look elsewhere and at least make a little money.

My family didn't know how to help me. Many times we

talked about what I should do. I could tell my family was reluctant for me to leave Christian work. Like Onesimus I had advice, but what was God saying? What should I do?

Scriptures are silent about Onesimus and his days or moments of deliberation as to whether or not he should listen to Paul and return to Colosse. I would like to think his faith was then strong enough to accept such a hard decision without much hesitation. But I am also human and fallible enough to suspect that the choice was as hard for Onesimus as it was for me and uncounted others when the time came to act.

Somehow, early in my Christian life I had gotten the impression that living for God was hard at first, but after a while it was easier, especially learning to find the Lord's will. I realize now how wrong I was!

## "Tell Peter"
### (Mark 14;
### John 21)

A rooster crowing that early morning in Jerusalem sent
spasms of painful remorse through Peter's soul.

Like a cry of alarm, the sound brought the fisherman to
his feet. Just at that moment, the man who was the
center of attention, the quiet man who stood bound at
the doorway of the High Priest's house, turned and
looked in Peter's direction.

The Galilean, Simon, once called Peter, had been
moving around in the huddle of people who were trying
to warm themselves around a charcoal fire.

The people were giving him no peace. Several tried to
associate him with the man on trial. His best deception
and his foulest oaths failed to convince them. But then the
sudden crowing of the cock made him turn his eyes
toward Jesus, and he wondered if the Master had heard it
too.

He was too far away to speak, but words were
unnecessary. The look was enough. They had both heard
it. And they both knew what it meant.

Pushing himself out of the crowd, he lurched toward
the street and broke into a run. Away from the crowd he
stopped. Breathing heavily and trembling, he leaned

against a building and covered his face. Peter's friends, writing much later about this moment, said that the staunch, boastful fisherman, who had sworn that he would never deny his Lord, "wept bitterly."

Peter had been nearly twenty-four hours without sleep except for a few naps in Gethsemane while Jesus prayed. Peter and his friends had departed from Bethany the morning before. After the two-mile walk into the city to the temple area, and after the day's celebration, he had come to the upper room with the rest of his friends to observe Passover with the Master as he had requested.

All day he had heard the talk of revolt rippling through the crowd. People were waiting to see what Jesus would do. Many hoped he was the Messiah, who would break the Roman eagle's grip on their land and people. Fear and hatred sent shudders through the crowd as all day the heavily armored Roman soldiers trooped loudly and rudely through the narrow streets.

Peter, of all the disciples, knew the most of what his Master was doing, yet it appeared he understood very little about how the Kingdom Jesus had been talking about would come. The idea of a Messiah who was subject to death was repulsive to him. He was ready to dispute anyone's word about that—even the Lord's.

The evening had ended with the emotion-filled Pascal meal in the upper room, where Peter had listened carefully to each word from his Lord. He recoiled, stunned by the Lord's quiet rebuke at his embarrassing remark about Jesus not washing his feet. He seemed to have a penchant for misunderstanding things, saying too much, doing or saying the wrong things at the wrong time.

During the prayer time in Gethsemane several hours later, heavy eyelids claimed him in sleep several times. He knew how important it was to stay awake for the Lord's sake, but it was so difficult! The Lord was right. The spirit was willing, but . . . .

The clatter of weapons jolted Peter awake. "Judas!
What are you doing here?" Peter asked. "Arrest Jesus?
Never!" Out came Peter's short sword. Again an
impetuous spirit ran ahead of reason and instruction and
off came the ear of Malchus, the High Priest's servant.

Again rebuke from the Lord, this time more severe.
Jesus then healed the wounded ear of that treacherous
pawn who had been bought by assassins and was coming
in the name of legality and righteousness. "What is
happening?" Peter wondered. Nothing seemed to make
sense.

At a distance, Peter followed the arresting party, first to
the house of Annas, where resided the real power of
the high priestly office. Though Annas had been deposed
by the Roman governor of Syria, foxy old Annas still
controlled the office through his son-in-law Caiaphas, the
puppet High Priest. Then, once Annas was satisfied,
the crowd moved on to Caiaphas' house.

Three times during the early morning hours, Peter had
been accused of being one of Jesus' followers. And
three times he had denied that he even knew him. That
was when the steadfast look of Jesus had fallen on
Peter, the denier.

That look must have stirred other thoughts within him.
Of all the people in the courtyard at whom Jesus might
have cast that soul-piercing look, it was upon Peter that it
fell. It could have signified that of all those present,
Peter was the one about whom Jesus was most concerned
at that moment.

Peter's night of weeping was long and dark. But now
light was breaking and his weeping was over. Scripture is
silent as to where Peter stayed during those hours when
Jesus was in the grave. Perhaps he was in the household
that had provided the Passover meal. One of the Gospel
narratives gives some indication that he was staying
at the same place where John was, the disciple who had

stood courageously at the foot of the cross with Jesus' mother and the other women. Peter probably wished he had been there with them. John's nearness during the silent period surrounding the Passover and Sabbath might have provided some comfort to Peter, one may imagine, but Peter's remembering John standing at the cross may have been cause for further self-castigation. Peter was glad at least that someone was with Jesus when the end came.

What awakened Peter on that early morning of the first day of the week? Was it the women's pounding on the door or their shouts? Their incredible story sent Peter and John running to the tomb. It was indeed empty, just as the women had said. Had Jesus' body been stolen, or had something Jesus explained earlier about rising again from the dead really come to pass?

All of Jerusalem would soon hear the news of the missing body. Each person would decide for himself whether to believe that the body had been stolen or whether a Messianic prophecy about resurrection had really taken place. Some would believe in the risen Christ and find hope, comfort, and release from the weight of their sin and guilt. Others would doubt and, in doubting, continue in darkness because of their own denial of truth and light.

Little by little the resurrection story was reconstructed as one witness after another brought new bits of information to the disciples. "Yes," the women said. They were sure that they had heard the angel at the tomb say, "Give this message to his disciples, including Peter." Yes, they were certain about the last part—Peter too.

As Jesus had instructed the disciples earlier, and as the angels restated his instructions, the disciples left for Galilee as soon as the religious festival was over. Galilee was the place they knew best, and they knew the Lord would come looking for them there, doing what they knew best—fishing.

In the early morning light, the disciples, returning to shore in their fishing boats, saw someone walking on the beach near the boat landing. And as the early morning mist lifted, they were reunited with their Lord, who had prepared a meal for them. The pleasant awe of being back in familiar Galilee was upon them, standing on the shore with their beloved Lord. Yet Jesus must have appeared somehow different to them. They must have sensed that he was not to be with them much longer, not as before, anyway.

This feeling that their remaining time with Jesus was short made his question to Peter, aimed at his uncertain heart, even more troubling. "Simon, son of Jonah, do you love me more than these others do?" Not once, or twice, but three times Jesus asked. It was concerning the volitional kind of love, *agapao*, that Jesus questioned. And three times Peter answered, "You know that I love you." But the kind of love he pledged was another verb, *phileo,* the kind of love and adoration that needs no urging or act of the will to perform, the love which is the overflow of a heart toward someone who is highly esteemed and lovable.

The lesson to Peter and the others was obvious. Peter's three denials needed abrogation by his three new pledges of love. And the Lord responded three times with commands, especially to Peter, to feed and nurture the flock. The one who had denied Jesus was becoming the shepherd and pastor of the frightened flock.

# NINE
## WAITING FOR GOD

Many afternoons as I was leaving the swelter of the city, I would think through the unfruitful employment interviews I had undergone during the morning. What more could I do? How would I improve my presentation? Sometimes a crossword puzzle was the escape I used to keep from thinking about the real puzzle before me, the bewilderment of why I was on this train, going home again in defeat instead of sitting in one of those tall buildings downtown, happy and usefully employed.

I wondered if Peter ever asked himself, "What if . . . ?" What would have happened had he chosen to stand with his Master and risk crucifixion at Jesus' side? What if Peter had bravely confessed, "Yes, I know him. I have stood with him and for what he believes for years now." What if . . . ?

What if I had done this instead of that—whatever it was that I thought at the moment may have been at the root of my failure that had caused me to have to give up my job? Had I acted differently, I might not be running back and forth to the city on hot days, sitting on the train looking for a five-letter word beginning with "E" that means "Made a mistake" to complete my crossword puzzle. Instead I would be seated in an office, busily making decisions about editorial projects, doing the fascinating work that had become as important to me as air and food and sleep. Think of anything, but don't think about that! It hurt too much.

Memories of my last job ran back and forth through my mind. It had been exciting, meeting authors and writers, stimulating their minds and being stimulated by them, seeking advice and being sought for advice.

Instead, I was now returning home from another pointless, fruitless interview, where I had again tried unsuccessfully to convince yet another possible employer that I was well worth the money he was going to spend to hire a competent editor.

At midafternoon the train was almost empty. There was no one near me in the coach to talk to, even about the weather. But the worst quietness was the silence from heaven. I would have settled for a few more phone calls from well-wishing friends.

For the first few months it had been easy to keep up courage. But soon it was obvious that personnel managers weren't lining up to ask for my resumé.

The months of indecision and doubt about my usefulness to the Lord made me more and more restless. One day, almost on impulse, I picked up the phone and called the office of a denominational headquarters across town. I doubted that any openings existed for a weekend ministry, and so did the church leader who politely answered my call. But, as he suggested, I sent a brief resumé of my experience for him to file just in case. Maybe in a few months or years a pastor miles away would call for someone to fill in for him for a week of vacation or illness.

Several days later a man twenty miles away picked up his telephone and dialed the extension division of a nearby Christian school to ask for someone to fill the pulpit of their small church that was trying to keep its doors

open. As the phone began to ring, he thought better of
the call, hung up, and dialed the denominational headquarters and spoke to the very person to whom I had
talked several days before. That man opened his file
drawer and pulled out my resumé, which had just arrived
in the mail, and read the information to the caller.

Later that morning my phone rang and I talked to the
chairman of the church board who asked me to fill in until they found a regular pastor. I didn't realize then that
the man with whom I spoke was dying, by that time almost too ill to attend services at the church. Nor did I
know how God would use that man and his church to
restore and rebuild me spiritually as I ministered to him
and his family and the little church, so burdened with discouragement.

Almost every family in the church was going through a
crisis of some kind, a spiritual or emotional separation because one spouse was a believer and the other wasn't, or
one or another family member was out of fellowship with
the Lord and bringing strife into the home. Nor did I
know, as I prepared the man for his death, just how
much of a resurrection was going on in my own life.

Many times during the next months, as I stood to
preach reconciliation to that small church congregation, I
wondered how long I would wait to know about my
friends, the people whom I had known at work, who still
seemed to hold me at arm's length. Whether they accepted me back, forgiven and emancipated, was a matter
completely out of my hands.

The people in the little church knew very little about
what had happened to me. I had explained the situation
to the church leaders, who accepted my explanation of
the problem and were satisfied with my desire to please
the Lord with my life. The acceptance I saw on their faces
each week would have to be my answer from the Lord
for the time being.

Reconciliation and healing might take a long time, I knew. I prayed about it often on the lonely drive home late each Sunday night.

The sense of usefulness helped me to see that results are measured in terms of God's values, often very different from our own. We tend to use all the wrong measuring sticks and become so concerned about meeting other people's expectations of us, when all God asks from us is that we do, each moment, what we know to be right.

One evening I again made the twenty-mile drive to conduct the midweek service at the small church. I talked about Simon Peter. "Poor vacillating Peter. Always saying too much, acting too hastily," we say. Yet every sin of every believer is equally a betrayal of what we know about God and his work in our lives. One does not have to know Jesus personally as Peter did, or hear a cock crow while he is being denied, to know that God hates sin. Peter himself attested later that God has "given us everything we need for life and godliness through our knowledge of him who called us by his own glory and goodness."

But some of our sins, through cultural manipulation, have come to be more acceptable, more respectable. We are quick to hear Peter's loud denial. Yet we are slow to hear our own voices raised to wound a fellow believer, whether in his presence or absence. We remember Peter's angry claim: "I never knew him!" But we forget the times when our lives, as seen by others, testify that we do not know him either.

I have often wondered what the results would show in polling a sizeable group of Christians about their attitude toward the relative "goodness" or "badness" of certain sins. For instance, what incidents from the life of Simon Peter would they recall most clearly? Would they remember the good things about him, or would they remember the bad? Would they recall the denial, the clumsy-sounding remarks, the attempt to defend the Lord by drawing blood from the High Priest's servant that night?

Or would the people remember Peter as the disciple who dared to climb out of a ship in the middle of the sea and try to walk on water?

> *They pulled him back*
>    *into the boat—*
>    *with pity? or with envy?*
> *He cried for help*
>    *before he sank,*
>    *in unbelief and terror.*
> *But yet he had,*
>    *however briefly,*
>    *bravely walked on water!*

Say what we will, Peter did what most of us only dream of doing. If only for a second or two, he walked on water—longer than any of his critics.

Who would remember Peter as the one who recognized Jesus as more than just a prophet? All the disciples did that, but Peter went farther in his claim. "Jesus asked, 'Who do you say I am?' Simon Peter answered, 'You are the Christ, the Son of the living God.' " He was the first to comprehend the difference between a courageous prophet like John the Baptist, or a suffering prophet like Elijah or Jeremiah, and Jesus as the Son of God.

In every listing of the disciples, Peter is mentioned prominently. When a spokesman was to come forward from a group, it was Peter. When an explanation was expected concerning the noisy language explosion of the believers gathered in the upper room on the day of Pentecost, it came from Peter.

Who can honestly rank people and their relative value and usefulness? Or who in the church today could dispute that on the Day of Pentecost, the most important man on earth, as far as the work of the Kingdom was concerned, was Peter? It was his testimony and faith that were the foundation rock of the Church that God was building, a man whose word became authority, as the authority of an official keyholder of a kingdom, as Christ said he was to be.

Yet this was the same man who, less than two months before the day of Pentecost, cowered in the early morning chill and stood next to a charcoal brazier, far more concerned with his physical comfort and safety than with anybody's kingdom.

For us those three days of Peter's life are genuinely silent days. We may enter into that kind of silence only through our own pain as we recognize ourselves, our own denials, our own failures to respond to the truth and light, and in the ensuing silence and tear-filled darkness that results from our failure.

Somewhere across this incredible chasm of inconsistency—a cowardly denier and the powerful Pentecost preacher and leader of the church—lies one of the most important lessons we can learn from the Scriptures about grace, forgiveness, restoration, and the power of the Holy Spirit.

After the service, instead of immediately going home I drove to the north side of town and stopped in front of a quaint little brick home, one that I had been in almost as much as I had been in my own home during the past few months. Upstairs lay my friend Bob, the deacon who had called me that first time to invite me to preach in the church. Bob's health was growing steadily worse from the cancer destroying his body, tearing him with pain.

His bright, liquid eyes were unforgettable. How remarkable that I could look straight into the eyes of this dying man and tell him how certain I was of God's love for both of us. We often talked about the previous

Sunday's message I had given at the church. One of
the women of the church had arranged to have the
sermons recorded and delivered to him the next day. The
Sunday sermons meant more to him than anything we
could do for him, he said. I thought it might be the
echoes off the walls of the church he loved coming through
on the tapes that were so meaningful to him. Not being
able to attend church seemed to him the worst part
of his confinement.

Was he really staying strong in spirit because of the
sermons on the tapes and from our visits, as he claimed?
Was I really feeding the flock, as he said? Or was he
just trying to reassure me that God was using me to
minister to him and to his family because he knew
how discouraged I had been about losing my job and
about not being able to find another? He had become my
most faithful parishioner and at the same time, except
for my wife Priscilla, my most valued confidante.

Bob told me often that he was praying for the Lord to
provide me with just the position God wanted me to
have, and in God's perfect time. Yet he said he hoped it
wouldn't mean my giving up the part-time pastorate
at his church. I assured him that it wouldn't.

Weekly visits to his house soon were broadened to two
or three visits a week, later once a day, and during the
last days, I spent many hours at his side. I wanted
very much to be with him when he slipped away, but the
Lord didn't allow it. As I was downstairs talking with
his wife, Helen, Bob was holding the hand of his daughter
Robin. By the time she called for us to come and we
had reached the top of the stairs, he was gone, his spirit
wafted away on the notes of a beautiful hymn playing
softly on the radio by his bed. By the time our tears came,
Bob's were already being wiped away by the Lord
whom he served, who had reached out and taken him
home.

The wind through the open windows fluttered the

funeral flowers in the church as it quietly filled up. Another wind blowing through my heart seemed to make much more of my well-chosen words than they themselves ever could have meant. Several dozen persons, Bob's friends and mine, their cheeks sparkling with tears at the loss of their friend, rose to rededicate themselves to the Lord whom Bob had loved so much.

There were no voices from heaven at the graveside. I heard only my own words being whipped about by the hot midsummer wind as church people stood around Bob's open grave. The sense of loss I felt for my friend made my voice sound forced and hollow. Yet within me was the joy of knowing that Bob's spirit stood not with us on that hillside, blasted by a hot prairie wind, but in the halls of heaven, where there is no more sorrow or pain.

Then it occurred to me that I, the uncertain, question-filled man speaking there—a being almost detached from myself—was the pastor of this flock. And God was using my words.

"Yes, Lord, you know that I love you," Peter had said. Denials of Christ and his power had been many—too many—and my lack of trust too controlling during the long, dark nights of my doubt.

But the message from the open tomb, the one Peter examined and found empty, and the one that I stood beside, was that Jesus wants to restore failures, those who thought they were failures, and send them back out to feed his flock.

# The Man Who Limped
## (Genesis 25—33)

Jacob stood alone, watching the last of Laban's caravan waver ghostlike, then disappear through heat waves rising from the sandy wasteland. Their meeting had been cold and threatening, but it ended calmly with their Mizpah covenant, committing Laban to stay at a safe distance to the north and Jacob to the south.

Grudgingly, the elderly Laban kissed his daughters and grandchildren good-bye, called his relatives together, and started home. His daughters, Leah and Rachel, stood with Jacob, getting their last glimpses of their blood relatives. The covenant forever closed the door to Jacob's family, now returning to Haran. Too many hard feelings and years of treachery had made the separation necessary.

Just as his grandfather Abraham had entered Egypt virtually a pauper and returned to his homeland a wealthy man, so Jacob was returning from Haran in fullness. Twenty years earlier, in fear of his life, he had left his father Isaac on the pretense of returning to his mother's homeland to seek a wife for himself. Everyone in Isaac's household, except perhaps the aging Isaac himself, knew that Jacob was fleeing angry Esau, his older brother. Esau had threatened revenge for Jacob's double

treachery, first for his tricky purchase of the birthright
and later for taking by deceit his father's deathbed blessing.

Though Esau's own passions had entrapped him, he
thought he still had reason to be angry. Returning from the
hunt, feeling like a half-starved animal, he had cared
more for a bowl of Isaac's red soup than for his sacred
birthright. That birthright encompassed not only the
firstborn son's larger inheritance but also moral and
spiritual leadership of the entire clan.

Knowing Esau's wild and undisciplined nature and lack
of discernment, as evidenced in his taking pagan wives,
his own mother Rebekah realized how unworthy Esau was
of his father's blessing. Through trickery she enabled
her favorite son, Jacob, the quiet, peaceable son, to obtain
the father's deathbed blessing by disguising Jacob in
Esau's clothing. Isaac, thinking he was talking to Esau,
gave Jacob the blessing he had intended for his older
son.

Esau, who had gone out hunting deer for his father,
returned to find he had been tricked again, causing him
to weep with an anguish that later turned to angry
threats. Twenty years later, obeying God's new marching
orders, Jacob was returning to his homeland. Had
Esau's anger dissipated over the years? Jacob needed to
know. As he broke camp at the place where he and
Laban had piled a heap of stones to seal their covenant
to stay away from each other, Jacob recognized that
ahead of him was an anger much worse than Laban's.

Behind him, an adversary sealed his path of return to
Haran. An arid wasteland lay on either side of him.
And an angry, threatening brother was somewhere on the
other side of the river, waiting for him.

The wealth accumulated in Paddan Aram through his
manipulation of Laban's flocks could help Jacob very
little at that moment. Herds of cattle, sheep, goats, and

donkeys, and the host of servants would mean nothing if
Esau's weapons ever found their mark.

Standing between the bitterness of past treacheries and
the terror of an unknown future, Jacob stood questioning
whether it was worth going on.

Jacob and his people stood between two camps—two
worlds—Laban's and Esau's, his past and his future.
He had time to think about how he had gotten himself
into such a position. He had had no choice but to
leave Beersheba twenty years before. Leaving an angry
brother behind him must have weighed heavily upon
him as he had hobbled the camels and had lain down in
his camp that first night at Bethel.

But alone in the desert God's angels had appeared to
him. In Jacob's troubled dream he had seen them
ascending and descending a radiant ladder from what he
took to be the very gate of heaven. "If God will be
with me and will watch over me on this journey . . . so
that I return safely to my father's house, then the Lord will
be my God" (Gen. 28:20). Even his vow had bespoken
his attitude to set the conditions on his own terms,
revealing his spirit's unwillingness to trust God unconditionally.

The following twenty years of plotting and being
plotted against were enough to soften Jacob, to prepare
him to hear God's voice again. This time the voice
called him to return to his homeland, the land promised
to his grandfather Abraham and his father Isaac. The
land was now to be his as the son holding the birthright.

Again Jacob stood in the wilderness on the other
side of the river Jordan from Bethel and again the angels
met him. As they had assured him on his departure to
Haran, so they met him again to reassure his safe return.

"When Jacob saw them [the angels], he said, 'This
is the camp of God' " (32:2). So he named the place

"Mahanaim," ("two camps"). Jacob was seeing visually what had been the unseen truth all his life. He could do his best to uphold his own cause, he could accumulate material gains through his own stealth. But the unseen camp of God's angels had been beside him all the time, giving and taking from him. A plan much bigger than his was unfolding. He had seen himself as being alone and self-sufficient, "snatching heels," as his name implied. But all the while a stronger hand than his was orchestrating a greater plan.

Word soon reached him that Esau was coming with four hundred men. It seemed as if Esau was sending a war party. Jacob had sent messengers offering most of his material wealth to Esau as a token of peace. But at that moment, with four hundred men behind Esau, there was no indication of what he had in mind.

Still scheming, Jacob divided up his camp so that at least one contingent might escape if Esau planned an ambush. Sending his family and servants across the Jabbok River, one of the streams that fed into the east side of the Jordan, Jacob returned to spend the night in prayer.

"So Jacob was left alone, and a man wrestled with him until daybreak" (32:24). Some have thought it to be the Son of God himself. In this brief narrative, Jacob becomes the paradigm of every person who has struggled with self-sufficiency and rebellion. He may have thought his worst struggle was with circumstances. God could just as easily have allowed him to proceed first from his mother's womb, and all his scheming for the birthright would have been unnecessary. He may have thought his biggest problem was his father, whom he had deceived, or his brother, whom he had defrauded, or his uncle Laban, whom he had practically impoverished. But all along, his struggle was with God. This wrestling match on the banks of the Jabbok was going to be a fight to the finish for control of his life. "Then the man said, 'Let me go, for it is daybreak' " (32:26). The fight had gone out of Jacob. The man who wrestled with him had given him a new name: Israel, "a prince with God." Now Jacob's proud look and self-assured strut were gone. This time he limped across the brook to meet his brother Esau.

The way back to the place of God's blessing had been hard. Limping and humble, the new man, Israel, struggled up the west bank of the Jabbok. Awaiting him was Esau, with an embrace and a kiss.

# TEN
# CROSSING OVER

I used to believe that fear was beneficial. I had genuinely wanted to believe this once when an army instructor, sounding very confident, told me that. We had just finished basic training and most of our training company was due to leave for the battlefront during the worst of the Korean conflict. I had every reason to believe that within a few weeks I would be among the front-line troops. I wanted to learn everything that would be of help to me should that time come.

Fear was supposed to be a good thing, he said. It caused the body to secrete extra adrenaline. The whole body—the hearing, sight, muscles—all would operate 30 percent more efficiently, he said.

But he didn't say that this kind of stress couldn't continue indefinitely. He didn't say that a long-term taxing of the system was what produced the condition called battle fatigue or shell-shock. He didn't say what this gnawing, drawn-out terror could produce when the human spirit is stretched to the limit and beyond for too long a period of time.

After basic training, I was assigned to a noncombat zone in Europe, so I didn't get shell-shock on the battlefield.

I learned about it those many years later in another,
also painful, way.

For more than six months after I lost my job, I did
some free-lance writing in my makeshift office at home—
a bedroom converted to a study. In jest, not meaning
me any pain or insult, a friend reminded me that being a
free-lance writer and editor was another way of saying
I was "unemployed." We laughed together at the truth of
it.

A recurring nightmare that had plagued me several
years before came back to haunt me. Several times I had
awakened half-sick with fear after dreaming that I had
somehow been horribly disgraced and had lost my job,
my family, and was living in a skid-row rescue mission,
unable to pull myself together again. Because my life at
that time had seemed to be going so well, I had
wondered why I ever dreamed such a thing.

Perhaps the dream was made up of bits and pieces of
memory of things I had seen years before. For several
years I had worked on a project with a group of students
who attended the college in western New York where
I was teaching. Several times a week we would drive to a
town about twenty-five miles from the college to operate
a coffee house. We were trying to attract some of the
teenagers who clogged the streets of that town each
weekend, looking for thrills and trouble.

One evening a fellow named Walter stumbled into the
coffee house. Years of heavy drinking and physical
abuse had turned his forty-four-year-old body into that of
a worn-out old man. Smelly and sick, he sat in the
overheated room and poured out the story of his failures
and of his losing battle with alcohol. He told of a family
he had lost; then, dropping his head onto the shoulder of
a tall freshman, the drunk began to sob. Wrapped in
the strong bear hug of this young man not half his age,
Walter cried himself quiet. Walter and Phil etched on my

mind an unforgettably poignant picture of Christian
love and caring—a big college freshman, hugging a worn-
out alcoholic for Jesus' sake.

The next time I saw Walter was late one night about
two months later. Drunk, and angered by the taunts
of several street-hardened teenagers, Walter reeled across
the sidewalk in front of a hamburger place, the teenagers'
hangout. Swinging wildly at one of them, he fell spread-
eagle and face down on the dirty sidewalk, just inches
from my feet. Propping him up on the curbstone and
sitting beside him, I talked to him, asking him when
he had last eaten anything.

"This morning . . . ?" He wasn't really sure. I went
inside and brought out a hamburger for him, and watched
him wolf it down in three hungry bites, hardly chewing
it. In a few minutes he was calm and nearly asleep.
The teenagers, now embarrassed, edged away one by
one.

In a few minutes Walter lurched to his feet, steadied
himself, and started off. He assured me that he was all
right. No, he could walk. He refused a ride in my car.
Off he stumbled to a nearby farm where he had been
living. Someone had given him an abandoned chicken
shed to live in.

Nearly ten years later, as I sat at my desk waiting for
free-lance work to come in, I thought of Walter several
times.

I wondered just what kind of smashing of my spirit it
would have taken for me to become like Walter.
How much despair does it take to put a human spirit into
such an irrevocable tailspin? For some reason, the
distance between us now seemed treacherously narrow. I
wasn't completely desperate; I lived in a nice warm
home, and my family was with me. And there was the
church where I ministered. But someone in despair looks
fearfully at the bottom of the spiral, to the likes of

Walter, and wonders how long it takes to get that far.

Being out of work for six months doesn't make anyone a failure. The worst failure I could inflict on myself, I reasoned, would be to lapse again into self-pity and make myself loathsome to those who kept offering me hope.

"Character grows in adversity," I once had heard. Not necessarily! Character can grow in adversity, or it can self-destruct. My patient, affirming wife reminded me of something important one day when I was thinking out loud about what was happening to my reputation. Some people are prone to think that a person who can't find work probably isn't very good at what he does or people would be looking for his skills. Her reminder was: "Reputation is what people think of you—character is what you really are inside."

Even Walter could have changed. His worst enemy was himself, his loss of faith in himself, which was blinding him to the possibility of God's transforming grace. The struggles Walter had, stuporous and slouching on the curbstone, and my despair at losing my job and subsequently losing faith in myself were different only in degree. And unless I would choose to believe in God and in his gracious willingness to respond to my own character decisions, I could with each passing day become more like Walter.

Our worst sins in this life are akin to Adam's choice to be self-sufficient and self-directed. God doesn't care much for the self-made man. The sin which approaches the sin of self-sufficiency and self-trust is that of refusing the all-sufficient God of grace. Both the refusal of God's grace and expecting God to do it all are decisions we make. The grace of God and the freedom of choice he has given to us become a theological contradiction only when we arbitrarily try to separate them.

Recently my neighbor received some good news. Her son, now well into manhood, called her from halfway

across the country to make his peace with her. Both of
them had felt bad about his difficult childhood and
his unhappy teenage years.

But that was a long time ago, and now he wanted her
to know that everything was all right between them.
She was especially glad to hear that he was getting his life
straightened out and had just been accepted into
graduate studies at a university.

As mother and son talked about the unpleasant past,
she asked him what had hurt him the worst—the
parents' divorce, the unhappiness in the home? What?

"It was getting expelled from school," he told her. "For
more than ten years I was bitter and angry and didn't
care what happened to me."

His mother agreed that her son had probably been
mishandled by the school leaders. Her son hadn't been
doing well in public school, so it was decided, with
the boy's agreement, that he should go to a local Christian
high school. He immediately got involved in their
athletics program and for the first time took a real interest
in school. He really loved the school, settled down,
and was looking forward to a good year. But then he and
some friends got into some mischief which the school
took as being very serious. His mother doubted that the
accusations against him were really all true, and even
if they were, his offense didn't seem serious enough to
warrant expulsion. When the young man was expelled
from school, he became bitter, withdrawn, and dropped
out of church, wanting nothing to do with Christians.
He later ran away from home and wasn't heard from for
more than five years.

But that was all in the past, and for both mother and
son it had to be forgiven and put behind them, which
they were able to do in that phone conversation. What
mattered most was that the bitterness which the son
had almost allowed to destroy him had been dealt with

and had been overcome and his life was back on track again.

Perhaps it shouldn't have taken ten years to recover. Of course, it had been wrong for him to become bitter in the first place, yet it was clearly understandable. How much better it would have been had there been someone to help him return home.

The little church I was pastoring proved to be as much a blessing to me as my work there seemed to be to the people. As healing came, I began to feel more and more at home as the shepherd of that small flock.

Doubts came and went, especially during the solemn moments—at the bedside of my dying friend, and later at the communion table as I stood there one Sunday. That morning I began to tremble inside. The preparation for the morning sermon had taken no more time than usual. But when I began to prepare the communion talk, a strange sense of uneasiness had come over me, and now as I stood to begin the communion message the sense of uneasiness returned.

Standing before the communion table reminded me once more of Aaron and how he must have felt standing before the ark of the covenant, looking up at the awesome glory cloud that stood over the ark. The incense in the censer that Aaron placed over the hot coals from the altar sent a heavy cloud of pungent smoke through the guarded chamber of the Holy of Holies.

The man who stood there in God's presence represented all men. Aaron had entered the office of priest because God had chosen him, not because he was good. His right earlobe had been anointed with the blood of the sacrifice, and his right thumb, and the big toe of his right foot. Ceremonially he was clean because God had accepted his sacrifice and anointing. The same anointing of the right earlobe, right thumb, and right big toe, first with blood and then with oil, was what God required

even of the lepers who were brought to the priest for
ceremonial cleansing so they could once again enter the
congregation of God's people.

From the lowest leper to the highest earthly priest, all
were defiled, and all could be made clean. The censer
and the vessel of blood of the sacrifice trembled in Aaron's
hands.

The deacons came forward and sat down beside me at
the communion table. The hushed congregation hung
on every word I read: " . . . Yet we considered him stricken
by God, smitten by him and afflicted. But he was
pierced for our transgressions, he was crushed for our
iniquities. The punishment that brought us peace was upon
him, and by his wounds we are healed" (Is. 53:4, 5).

Could any of them really know how I felt? Did they
have any idea how deep I had plummeted into
depression such a short time ago? Did they really know
the leprosy of self-deprecation I had invoked upon myself?

One of the deacons, a man I knew who, like me, had
many needs for which he and I had been praying,
rose to offer thanks for Christ's broken body.

I read, "We all, like sheep, have gone astray. We have
turned every one to his own way; and the Lord has
laid on him the iniquity of us all" (53:6). Could any of
them listening to me really understand that the tear
on my cheek was due to more than the high emotion of
that sacred moment?

The other deacon, himself a struggler like me, whose
family had seen days of troubled relations, offered a
prayer for the cup. One by one the people took the
emblem of Christ's blood. There was no fear in any
of their faces. It was to them a cup of hope, taken slowly,
deliberately, gratefully.

The deacons returned to the front and sat down by the
communion table. I took the tray and served them.

Behind the table again, I reached for one of the little
vessels filled with pungent grape juice. The cup trembled
in my hands as I lifted it to my lips and drank. Then I
stood in silence for a few moments, thinking about blood
and forgiveness, about lepers and priests. Opening my
eyes, I saw the congregation, misty-eyed, waiting, perhaps
grateful for the long pause, but waiting for the benediction.

On impulse I turned to the Book of Hebrews. I had
intended another benediction, but instead I wanted to read
those words from the last chapter, words I had come to
treasure. Struggling with my emotion-filled voice, and
seeing through tear-filled eyes, I read:

*May the God of peace, who through the blood of the
eternal covenant brought back from the dead our Lord
Jesus, that great Shepherd of the sheep, equip you
with everything good for doing his will, and may he work
in us what is pleasing to him, through Jesus Christ, to
whom be glory for ever and ever. Amen* (Heb. 13:20,
21).

The God of peace sent us on our way that morning,
and we were aware that we stood not in our own
righteousness but in his, not in our own garments but in
his provision for us in Christ.

I left the church that morning more aware than ever
that it was God's work of forgiveness that would equip me
to do his will, that the glory was his for ever and ever.

One morning when the alarm went off and my wife got
up to start breakfast, I still hadn't been asleep. I had
worked late, going over two red notebooks. One was
crammed with clippings, pamphlets, letters—samples of
the work I had done over the past ten years, a portfolio I
had put together to show would-be employers. The other
notebook, growing fuller every day, was a logbook of

resumés mailed out, calls I had made, classified ads I had answered, and appointments with my employment counselor. Out of all those contacts, or from at least one of the letters sent out, it seemed that at least one positive answer should have come. The wrestling went on and on.

It was not the finger of God in the hollow of my thigh as Jacob experienced, but all the pain and feeling of impotence that was upon me. With the light of dawn came the truth of the real struggle going on. Until God blessed with his answer, there was nothing I could do but to hang on, like Jacob. "I will not let you go until you bless me," Jacob answered.

Breakfast was over and I finished cleaning up the kitchen. Priscilla was by now on her way to work. Opening the red notebooks again, I flipped each page, reminiscing about each of the projects represented by the clippings and brochures. I felt another surge of pride at each of them. Others had praised these efforts of mine also. Couldn't some of the would-be employers see the quality embodied there?

I tried to imagine what such a book would look like to a stranger seeing it for the first time. And what would I look like, sitting across the desk from the potential employer as he read it. How nervous did I look? How did my well-thought-out and well-rehearsed presentation sound to him—to the angels? How long would I have to hang on?

The phone rang. It was the personnel director of a Christian publisher, telling me about an opening they had for an experienced book editor. He said they had already called my former employers. This man knew me— who I was, why I had left my former job. He said he thought he understood the circumstances and that they wouldn't go against my chances of getting the job.

I dressed quickly, praying quietly with each button on

my shirt. Pulling my tie into a careful knot, I hurried toward the study and stood in front of the desk, thinking through what I needed to take with me. I picked up the resumés and the red notebook. The sight of the bright red cover was almost embarrassing to me now. I put them back on the desk and headed for the car, empty-handed.

The company already knew me—"all about me," he said. He smiled, shook my hand, and beckoned me to a chair. Perhaps he could see how badly I was limping.

# The Sinful Woman
## (Luke 7:37-50)

Jesus knew his audiences well. It was to such burdened
people that his message of comfort fell in words as
pleasant to the ear and as uplifting to the heart as a fragrant
spring breeze: "Come unto me, all you who are weary
and burdened, and I will give you rest. Take my yoke upon
you and learn from me, for I am gentle and humble in
heart, and you will find rest for your souls. For my
yoke is easy and my burden is light" (Matt. 11:28-30).

In the crowd a troubled woman was listening to his
message. In the words of Jesus, the troubled woman heard
a message of hope and forgiveness and accepted the
forgiveness of God that was being offered to her.

Perhaps she was standing in a doorway or by a village
well when she was touched by these words, so light
and fresh to the heart, the kind of words that would send
shockwaves through the hearts of those who were
holding on to stony, cold, traditional religiosity.

Somehow the woman learned where Jesus was, and
breaking into the dining room of Simon the Pharisee's
house, she fell sobbing at Jesus' feet. It was an unheard-
of breach of decorum.

The message about laying aside the heavy burden in

exchange for Christ's yoke may have been as troublesome to Simon the Pharisee as it was comforting to the sinful woman and the others who had heard Jesus. To learn more about the strange new teaching, Simon had requested Jesus' presence for dinner at his table.

But when the woman appeared and cried and wiped Jesus' feet with her hair, Simon suggested by his whispers that everyone should by now have heard about her reputation. The host was quick to recognize her for what she was, or at least for what she had been. It settled in his mind what he wanted to know about Jesus and his message: "If this man were a prophet, he would know who is touching him and what kind of woman she is—that she is a sinner" (Lk. 7:39).

Jesus said, "Simon, I have something to tell you." Then Jesus told Simon and his guests a parable of two sinners:

*"Two men owed money to a certain moneylender. One owed him five hundred denarii, and the other fifty. Neither of them had the money to pay him back, so he cancelled the debts of both. Now which of them will love him the more?" Simon knew the answer: "The one who was forgiven most." Then Jesus asked him: "Do you see this woman? I came into your house. You did not give me any water for my. feet, but she wet my feet with her tears and wiped them with her hair. You did not give me a kiss, but this woman, from the time I entered, has not stopped kissing my feet. You did not pour oil over my head, yet she has poured perfume on my feet. Therefore, I tell you, her many sins have been forgiven—for she loved much. But he who has been forgiven little loves little"* (7:41-47).

Then Jesus said to the woman, "Your faith has saved you; go in peace" (7:50).

# ELEVEN
# SPRING COMES AGAIN

It was a warm day and the car windows were down. I
recognized the middle-aged man several hundred feet
ahead before my car came abreast of him. He was
hurrying along the sidewalk, on his way to lunch. So was
I. But we were coming from different offices, he from
the place where I used to work and I from my new job. I
tapped the car horn and waved at him.

He smiled weakly and returned the wave. I was relieved
at my own feelings. Several months earlier I would
have relished a chance to remind him of the hurt he had
brought me. I would have wanted to stop the car,
grab the man by the collar and shout at him that I was
innocent of the things he believed about me, and that he
had been unfair in the way he dealt with me. But
today I did not find even a trace of anger in my heart.

Signs of springtime were everywhere. I felt it even inside
me. The warm sun was delightful and the new growth
of budding trees a pleasant reminder of how much healing
had taken place within me.

Genuine forgiveness brings a depth of healing that
removes the need for vindication. I realized that my
friend—at least, I wanted to be his friend—may never

completely understand what happened to me or what he
had done to hurt me. Nor would he know everything
that had happened in my heart and mind since the day I
left his office in such disgrace. He may never know
the part of the wrong I had accepted or what attempts at
restitution I had made. Perhaps he would always
believe that he had been right in asking me to resign.

But now, basking in the warmth of a spring breeze
whipping through the car window, I could forget all
that. The look on the man's face told me that nothing
had yet changed in his mind. God had changed me. He
could change my friend too. But seeing him and
thinking through my own reaction confirmed that at least
my part of the burden was gone.

There is no burden so heavy as the one laid upon us
by our fellowman. Simon the Pharisee and his self-
righteous friends, it would seem, made merchandise of
their own self-acclaimed righteousness by lording it
over those sinful outsiders who listened to their endless,
burdensome pronouncements of how hard it was to
please God. Simon's attitude, as we read about it in Luke's
record, sounded much like the other Pharisees about
whom Jesus warned on numerous occasions.

For the woman, kneeling at Jesus' feet, more was
falling than her tears. She was ridding herself of the burden
of sin that she had been bearing.

Many times I had wished for such a moment of release
as this woman experienced, a pinpoint in time when I
might sense a burden of sin falling from me, as John
Bunyan's Pilgrim had sensed it. The sinful woman
whom Luke told about was so aware of the work of grace
done on her behalf that nothing could have restrained
her overflow of gratitude and the tears that anointed Jesus'
feet.

Like her, I had felt the galling weight of failure. I had
wallowed helplessly in self-pity, giving in to bitterness

and depression. But little by little, God's healing breath had touched me, through his comforting Word and the helpful friends he sent to me. Without hearing or seeing the weight fall, the sudden awareness that the burden was completely gone surprised me. Now my mind pulled me back to attention and to the fact that I was in my car, on the way to meet friends at a nearby restaurant.

Healing often goes on best when it is least noticed, I had learned. My brothers and I grew up in South Carolina where mosquitoes kept our bare legs speckled with red welts. Barefoot, and in short pants, I was usually more concerned about fly balls or fish bait than with insect bites. Unconsciously I would scratch the mosquito bites and cause them to become infected. I took many scoldings from angry parents: "If you don't stop scratching those sores, they're never going to heal."

The healing of the soul is sometimes like the healing of insect bites. The more we think about and scratch our wounds or worry about what has happened or how unjustly we think we have been treated, the worse the sores become.

Perhaps in the past I had been attacking my problem the wrong way. Without realizing what I was doing, I was expecting others to realize how wrong they had been about me. When they were ready to admit they had been mistaken, then I could forgive myself for my failure to keep out of trouble. I was ready to admit my part in the failure, realizing I had put myself in a compromising situation which some people were bound to misunderstand. But in my anger and bitterness, I felt people had not been fair with me. I thought that once others had forgiven me and I had forgiven myself, then I would feel I could approach the Lord for the reassurance of his forgiveness.

By then I had more or less given up ever being vindicated by the ones who had lost confidence in me. I

learned to ignore those feelings, turn the problem
over to the Lord, and go on with my work.

The opportunity the Lord gave me to work with the
little church and the warm, reaffirming church people helped
me get over being angry. At what exact point the burden
and sense of worthlessness had disappeared, I may
never know. I just realized that spring day, driving through
town, with warm breezes whipping through the window,
that I didn't hurt inside anymore.

I should have realized, like the woman Luke wrote
about, that Jesus is the one who removes burdens, not
other people. She saw Jesus through the doorway
as he reclined in Simon's dining room and in she went!

We don't know much more about Simon than we
know about the woman who burst into his home unan-
nounced that day. If Jesus had been teaching in Simon's
village, it would appear that Simon was the town's
chief Pharisee. It was the custom in that day that the
senior rabbi should show hospitality to a visiting rabbi. Not
to invite an itinerant teacher into his home would have
been a breach of etiquette. It was likely in this case
that the occasion was used primarily to examine the
teachings of the traveling rabbi.

But Simon, going through the motions of providing
hospitality, proved to be no more sincere than some of
the other shallow Pharisees of that day. The Pharisees
were apparently more concerned with the outside appear-
ance of things than with the reality within.

Good manners would have provided a kiss of greeting
as Jesus entered the home. Simon had somehow
managed to forget this nicety. Good manners would have
provided a servant to wash Jesus' feet. Simon didn't
do that, another breach of custom. Good manners would
have provided a fragrant anointing oil for the head of
the guest. But Simon was concerned primarily with ap-
pearing to be hospitable and very little about how well

the guest was actually treated. We can be sure that Jesus was well aware of why he was there. Nevertheless, he came as a polite guest and took his place on the couch provided for him at the table.

According to custom, as the diner reclined on the couch, his feet would have been pointed away from the table. If the table was crowded, the woman would not have been able to reach Jesus' head, which may explain why she anointed Jesus' feet instead of his head.

Before anyone realized that she was near, she had already entered the door. Perhaps she intended only to anoint him with oil from the small alabaster vial she carried on a string around her neck, as women did in those days.

For some reason she decided against anointing his head but looked instead to his feet, which would have been nearer to her. How much relief must have overwhelmed her! How weighty a burden must have fallen! Only the abundance of tears from a heart overcome with emotion, gratitude, and humility could measure what she was feeling toward this One who had released her from such a burden of sin and guilt!

With nothing to wipe the overflow of tears, she removed a pin from her hair and let the heavy tresses unwind softly onto his feet. Then she began to use her hair as a towel to wipe her tears from his dusty feet. Lifting the vial of precious ointment, she broke it open and poured it on him.

How would one use such oil anyway? Some times drop by drop the fragrant contents would be released from the narrow neck of the vial. But in a sudden burst of celebration she broke the neck of the soft alabaster stone bottle and the entire contents were poured out as an anointing.

Not a word was said. Her quiet sobs and tears served a richer eloquence, as did the silent submission of Jesus to her unusual act of worship and expression of gratitude.

Simon also watched silently. His quiet rage was understood by Jesus. He "knew what was in a man" (Jn. 2:25). Simon thought, "If this man were a prophet, he would know who is touching him and what kind of woman she is" (Lk. 7:39).

Luke left so many questions unanswered—foolish questions, because the Holy Spirit answered all we really need to know of the Pharisee Simon and the sinful woman. "How did Simon come to know this woman?" we might ask. "Did he have some dark secret dealings with her? How did she know how to find Simon's house?"

Thousands and thousands of historical events were never recorded and yet Luke leaves this story to us. How poorly, like Simon, we see ourselves sometimes!

The Gospel writer Luke told us only a little of the woman's character. He was explicit, yet discreet. He told us only what we need to know of the delicate subject. He said she was "a woman who had lived a sinful life in that town" (7:37). That is all we know of her and all we need to know.

One special truth comes out of this story as a strange indictment, an accusation that Simon never realized would still stand against him two thousand years later. How sad that he, who knew this miserable woman and all about her sinful past, was either helpless or unwilling to do anything to free her from her burden of sin. How sad that he felt it his duty to lay even heavier burdens of hate and rejection on her and those like her!

How smug and righteous the man I waved at on my way to the restaurant had seemed that day nearly two years before as I left his office. He seemed to believe without question the story he had heard. His forceful language that day convinced me immediately that nothing I might say would change his mind. It was over. I would have to resign.

For days after I left his office, anger had gripped me so
tightly that at times I could scarcely breathe. How could
they do such a thing to me? How could God allow
it? Was I the first person who had ever had to undergo
this kind of shame? Certainly not, but the comfort other
people bring is no comfort at all, however prone we
are to seek others who have undergone similar injustices.
Swapping stories with other unfortunates only fertilizes
and nurtures bitterness.

Days of depression had followed, and my misery began
to fan out to others. Fortunately the Lord helped me to
recognize the effect my so-called "pity parties" were
having before I became loathsome to friends who had
stuck by me during those days.

For many months a deadly cycle had continued within
me as bad as the sin of Simon the Pharisee. Like him, I
found it hard to love and forgive others. I couldn't forgive
and love them because I hadn't yet accepted God's
forgiveness myself. I first had to learn what the sinful
woman had learned, that love to others is, as much
as anything else, an overflow of our love for Christ. It is
our gratitude for sins forgiven.

If the woman had waited until Simon the Pharisee had
forgiven her and recognized God's work of grace in
her life, she would likely have remained outside his house
forever, a sinful, uncertain woman. Simon and all the
other "righteous" Pharisees didn't know much about
releasing people's burdens, only how to place heavier
burdens on them by reminding them of how sinful they
were.

I had it all backward. First I had to reckon with God's
offer to lighten my burden. When that was gone, I
could then make my way past the Simons who still accused
and held grudges, and go to Jesus' feet with my tears.

We know very little of that woman from that moment
on. Some believe she was Mary Magdalene, who had

devils driven from her. Regardless of who she was or what
Simon and his righteous friends might have thought,
she knew who she was and what she was—a forgiven
sinner. She left that day a freed woman.

I would like to believe it was a beautiful day when she
left Simon's house. Whether it was sunny or dark,
somehow she must have known her life would be different
because a seal of forgiveness had been placed on her
at Simon's table. When Jesus says we are forgiven, we
are!

Before I realized it, my car was pulling into the restaurant
parking lot. I had been so deep in thought that I was
hardly aware of where I was. My mind had been on the
man I had passed a few minutes earlier, wondering if
he was aware of how the two of us stood before the Lord.

The parable of the two sinners was about us, really.
We were both the ones who had owed more than we
could ever pay. We had both been released from debts
too heavy for either of us to pay. We were the ones about
whom Jesus asked, "Which of them will love him more?"

Switching off the ignition, I saw through the restaurant
window the people whom I was meeting for lunch.
They had already found a table and were waving their
greetings, motioning me inside to where they were
already deeply involved in animated conversation.

I was eager to join them. I hadn't seen a couple of
these men for quite a while. Being back in touch with the
Lord made it easier now to be with them. The warm,
knowing looks and smiles, and their comments, "It's good
to see you, Wight!" were appreciated.

These were all good men, yet each in his own way
could someday get careless and fall as I did. I know also
that until I was securely in the sinless presence of
God, I was still subject to Satan's traps if I got careless
again.

We didn't talk much about those matters, but I imagined

all of us were thinking about my failure and recovery.
It was good to be back in touch with them. Our waitress
soon set steaming plates of food in front of us. My
friend across the table asked, "Does anyone want to thank
the Lord for all this?"

I really wanted to be the one to pray. Thanks for "all
this" probably meant more to me than just the food
in front of us. But I was afraid that my voice would become
too emotion-filled. I bowed my head and listened to
my friend.

It was a simple prayer—thanks for the food, and thanks
for the Christian friends—both gifts of God that I knew I
never again wanted to be without.